Ballad of a Bagpiper

To Sue

Watch out for falling sheep!

cheers

By

E A Channon

Strategic Book Group

Strategic Book Group

P.O. Box 333
Durham CT 06422

www.StrategicBookClub.com

ISBN:978-1-60976-497-5

PREFACE

I want to thank you for taking the time in reading this book. When it comes to the history of bagpipes that's just too long of a story and too many people have gone over this history already. This book is unlike any other book about bagpipes you have ever read. It's not about a famous bagpiper's story, well actually it is to a degree, or how certain piobreachds are played, that's Bach music style in the piping world. Though I have played the bagpipes for countless events whether military, friends or family wedding or even funerals, not just in Scotland but around the world. I'm not going to talk about my military experiences in the British Army, which just too weird and just can't be told, the United States Army or bagpipe bands in which I have been involved, it's just too boring and too long. I have done many amusing and amazing things with this weird sounding instrument that sound like a dead cat and looks like an octopus, so I hope that you find some of them as funny as I remember. Of course, coming from people that are known for their ability to drink as well as being thrifty spenders, scots have the knack for finding great humour in life.

From Europe to the United States and to Asia, I've played, seen, and done so many things because of this wonderful instrument including playing over 300 weddings and events. I've had the opportunity over the years to play for some well known and some not so well known people. One thing that always amazes me is discovering a person's feeling towards the bagpipes, half having the general opinion of liking this loud and unusual instrument, and the others half either don't but have a certain opinion about them at all or can't stand them. Yes this instrument is loud, but give it a chance! At weddings, parties and such arena of celebration the clatter of joy will only increase with this supposed noise.

The bagpipes brought together my wife and I and it has also brought me great sadness in the loss of my best friend in September of 2004. I also would like to say that of course for personal reasons I won't say the names of the people actually involved in the stories I relay in this book, so if your are a bride and groom that I have preformed for no worries. I do hope that some of these people might read this book and remembering the events mentioned here, pause to reflect and laugh about what happened because now they are looking at it from the outside in.

My wife and I had done weddings together for over six years when I was asked to start writing down what I've seen and done when it comes to the this great instrument. So with a laptop, paper, and many, many hours of doing research, racking my brain and cups of coffee from Starbucks, Tully's, Costa, Coffee Bean and more I finally sat down and started writing down what I had done.

So how does a person start writing about their life when it comes to playing the bagpipes at weddings, parties and such? It's not really that hard when I thought about it. I just sat down and started to write my experiences down many of these were experiences that a lot of pipers in the world could only dream about many I hope they don't. Through all the events that I have been paid to do, it was never the money that I was after. I've never really charged high prices for my services because I was out there for the fun of playing the pipes and seeing the joy it brought to people. It wasn't until I met my wife that I started or made by her really to charge a certain amount, what she said was an amount that professionals deserved.

Now I'm not the most experience piper or the most famous piper in the world and thank god for that. I'd hate to be the gentleman that plays for the queen every morning or the gentleman that plays for the chief of the Clan MacLeod at Dunvegan Castle in Scotland. I just happened to be at the right place at the right time, like meeting my wife during a wedding, but I also seem to have the incredible knack of getting into trouble, either due to the kilt, the accent or both giving me some great stories to share. I do hope you enjoy and get some laughter out of them. I sure do and man am I a nut sometimes.

Chapters

IN THE BEGINNING!

So like everyone I was born, but I was born into a family that had aristocratic beginnings from Cumbria, Cambridgeshire and Dorset. My family history included an ancestor that invented the water closet or what is called now the bathroom. He gave it as a present to Queen Elizabeth I for her birthday, and man what a present that must have been! "Here you go your majesty, a place that you can go shit in private".

This family also is famous for being in many battles throughout English and Scottish history, Henry 'Chips' Channon who helped Britain during World War 2, a few family members in the British Parliament and a football star. The most interesting part of the Channon history is ours family's crest. Got to love a family that has a woman's scalp, red head too, held by two arms as part of their crest, something I didn't share with my wife for many years due to her flaming red hair. They'll get far I think. There's a history about that crest but that's for later.

Things were a wee bit hard for me and my younger sister to get away with or do growing up. Things like getting by with not practicing our lessons whether it be the piano, school or chores around the house, never giving us a lot of free time to run around the neighborhood. Probably why today I am a wee bit more of a child when it comes to having fun. My parents were hard on us, but fair. It allowed me to become the bagpiper I am today, fair to people but also understanding on where people come from. My father was in the Navy and other military branches which meant we moved almost everywhere the British and American governments had bases, and my mother was a teacher of music in the local primary schools hence the reason they were both incredibly hard on us, making us both spend a lot of time practicing our music or to be a proper gentlemen and lady. My mum's part German, part Scottish, so when thinking back I always think she was strict like most German's are with things. "Practice, Practice, Practice" she would also say to us, sometimes hitting me with a ruler. I always saw something else though, getting easily distracted. My younger sister Liz was born four years after me making it, at first cool to have a younger sibling. Like everyone we had a fun growing up together, but like all siblings we also had fights here and there. One time I can remember on a plane to see my German grandmother, my sister in a fit of anger over something I was teasing her about, (it's ok I deserved it), took a model metal plane that the airline had given her and stuck it in my head, "ouch" is not the word I was thinking about. Blood everywhere, the plane had to land at a different airport and the other passengers giving us hateful looks. Even today I still have the scar on my head. Lucky girl though, because if something like that had happened today she might have been a guest at Guantanamo Bay. Plus this is probably why the toy planes are plastic today. I got her back later however, I stuck her in the dryer once, so much fun!

I went to normal schools, some private some not so private, but because my father was in the military we moved all over the place and I never stayed at one school too long. I can still remember one house I lived in on an Indian Reservation in New Mexico where a Native American boy, the chief's son, while playing thought we try to scalp each other just for fun. I mean we actually did try to scalp one another. Your thinking that must have hurt, well of course it did but I have a hard head, just ask my wife! I came running home to my mum crying with blood running down my face and a piece of my scalp flapping in the wind. I can only imagine what my parents thought, as my mum promptly passed out right in front of me. My dad taking me in the bathroom and washing me off before we went to the hospital. Got to be presentable in public, I guess.

Being part of a musical family it was easy for me to make contacts to play for weddings and other such things from an early age. My father plays the organ and piano and had been playing for as long as I could remember. He was trained at Salzburg University in Austria. He joking used to say he learned while sitting on top of Mozart while he practiced. He still plays the organ at his local church when he has time. As does my mother who still to this day teaches youngsters the art of playing the piano even having recitals twice a year boring the hell out of the kids parents each time.

My parent's musical knowledge and love of everything classical, medieval and ancient led to my first album being JS Bach, which shaped my life in such a way that music was always going to be a strong part of my life. This education I received from them included giving me an early taste of music by learning the piano. I tried and tried, but I couldn't play as well as they did, and soon fell behind in the many concerts that my mother gave over the years. It was just not for me, being stuck in one room for many hours, just not my cup of tea. My grandfather whom I first learned about the bagpipes from, told me once that there are two distinct differences between the bagpipes and the piano. The bagpipes first were older than the piano, making it one of the oldest instruments in the world behind the drum and voice. The other was if you suck at playing the piano you can't leave the room because the dam thing is so big while the people are throwing apples and eggs at you. I saw it happen once! With the bagpipes you can at least walk out and leave the room, which was excellent. I've heard some pipers over the years play on Princes Street in Edinburgh, Scotland and in harbor area in front of the Empress Hotel in Victoria, Canada and I really wished they did just that, walk away.

When I decided to play the pipes it was at a young age after spending those many hours stuck to the piano but I didn't really think that I'd be making a career of it at the time or anything of the sort when I was young. It was just something to do and it got me way from the piano. After a trip to England and Scotland to see family there, I was introduced to this great instrument that would change my life. This decision came after seeing my grandfather one day walking down the beach with this strange instrument on his shoulder playing this haunting music that drifted my way. My Grandfather had a fabulous history himself as does his bagpipes. He played for the Black Watch and landed at Normandy on D-Day during the fighting in Europe.

My grandfather who at this time was an Episcopal minister, would tell me about the glories of the Scottish regiments that conquered the world for the British crown and how the bagpipes made history where ever they went in the world. He was from the Dorset area of England, where most Channon's are from in our lineage and told me story after story of what Scotland had been like, almost making it a fantasy for me. So ever since then, around 5 years old, it became my life's dream to play this instrument, which happened of course later that year. However I found that living in New Orleans at the time, a part of the US that was almost anti-British, being a large French area of America it was very hard to find people to teach me. So I started to learn on my own and ended up doing very well at it myself. When visiting my grandfather back in Britain these times were special not only because it was time with him hearing the many stories of Scotland yet again, hence my love of history but it was also intense lesson after lesson with him which added to my learning experience. This is were my joy for playing for people came from, which is the key to my existence now, thus preserving the enjoyment and the beauty of this instrument even when in this modern day it is still considered an instrument of war in the United Kingdom.

Many beginners playing the pipes don't have a problem being shy for you are usually learning to play in front of hundreds of people at competitions such as highland games or with bands usually within the first year of starting up the pipes. Not me! It took a while for me to get used to it several years in fact, and sometimes depending on who I'm playing for, I was almost shitting in my pants, or kilt really. Such as when I played for the Queen or Princess Diana and there are a few others I still get a wee bit nervous about playing for. I admit I am a perfectionist and don't like to play a tune unless it's perfect. For shyness or performing they say that if you think of people naked you can get through anything, not me, it never did work when I played. Playing for some of the most important people in this world was both an honor and is very taxing on my nerves so how do you picture the Queen naked, ahhhhhh. It is just is not done.

One reason it took me longer to get used to learning and playing the pipes was the amount of learning disabilities I have had to overcome, many were not discovered until much later in my life. Even today I still have problems with my disabilities, such as dyslexia, not normal dyslexia either, well if anything is normal about it or if you can call dyslexia normal to any degree. I've got an extreme case of it, especially with numbers, seeing numbers upside down giving me problems even doing math in my mind. I can read a book at a normal pace however I can't remember what I've read most of the time as soon as I reach the end of the page, meaning that I will have to read things two or three times to retain their meaning.

This also happens when I try to read or learn music which becomes twice as difficult with the bagpipes as the music has to be memorized, no sheet music can be carried while your walking or rather marching, very hard unless you have a third arm. I can learn music quiet easily but can't remember how to play it ten minutes later. I can read and talk, but I guess the messages that go from the brain to the mouth get messed up, making speech sometimes even very hard and embarrassing, unless I concentrate. This is why I have used humor to a certain degree in my life however with the bagpipes there is no need, they carry the conversation for themselves.

I also received the gift of Attention Deficit Disorder which was diagnosed when I was around 10 years old making it even harder for me to learn things because I couldn't sit still for longer than a few minutes. I would get bored, probably why the piano was so hard to take, making me want to do something else because I hear, see, or smell something that might be more fun, so I leave. Hate it! Still today I have to concentrate to get through things. If you ask my wife, she'll says it complicates even our holidays to this day for they are never the relaxing sit on the beach type, always on the go that's me but it has led to some great adventures for the two of us around the world. I find it entertaining to take her to the many place I have lived and visited over the years, if nothing else then to see her reaction.

Over the years I've been discriminated against because of my disabilities, especially when dealing with universities. It has been a struggle to achieve the schooling that I have. One university I attended in the US had the best disability office that I can remember. They were able to deal with my disabilities, even helped me work through them. My disabilities, many caught so late in life, have made it hard to just learn a technique once on how to overcome, the struggles are constant and need constant assistance. I have found that a number of universities I have attended since, both in the US and UK, are unable to handle many disabilities a specially not someone with multiple disabilities, even to the point that I failed classes because the teachers, staff, and the disabilities office didn't know how to handle students with my problems and weren't trained right. I ended up having to fight to get anything done. Oh I hate being the test subject in things don't you? However this seemed to be the case with most of my education fighting to get anywhere. Over the years I've tried to fight and help children who have these disabilities that have dragged my life around. Its the least I can do.

Yet another problem that I've experienced over the years is when I wore my kilt. It's a piece of Scottish history, however to some, just clothing. Once, in order to celebrate St. Andrews Day while living in New England, I decided to wear my kilt to school. Since you can't find good haggis in the U.S., wearing a kilt was the next best thing. So I walked to school, which I did everyday, wearing my Donald Clan kilt and went to my classes. At lunch time, a teacher came up to me and asked me to go to the head teacher's office, which I did. I got there wondering what I might have done.

This school didn't have a dress code and I was wearing something under my kilt, which would bring me bad luck, but I didn't want to get arrested or upset someone at school. So I waited. The head teacher brought me into his office and we talked for about half and hour. With him asking me things like, "Why are you wearing a dress to school son?" I replied, "This isn't a dress; it's called a kilt and in Scotland it's their national dress, sir." The Head Master's response was, "This isn't Scotland." I love that response. To me, that's how simple minded a person is, as well as a cop-out for not understanding something. The Head Master went on to say, "And wearing that dress here to school has disrupted your classes and brought chaos to this school." He got up and walked over to lay his hand on my shoulder then, said, "Son," (I hate it when people called me that) "I understand why you want to wear it but if you don't take it off, I'm going to have to suspend you for the rest of the day." Well, I took the suspension and came back to school with no worries in my mind the next day. I felt strongly about wearing my kilt and that I had done nothing wrong. Why do other cultures get to wear their national clothes? So why can't a Scotsman wear his? I was thinking this when I was called again to go to the main office, but this time it was to see the psychiatrist. I had never seen one before so this was a wee bit scary for me. I got into his office and sat down not really understanding why I was there. He started by saying, "So I was informed that you are wearing dresses. Now what can you tell me about this son?" I explained what I had worn was a kilt and went into the history of it, expressing in a strong way that I was not wearing a dress. The meeting only took about fifteen minutes but I left being told that he was going to watch me the rest of the week and talk to me again in the future. He never did talk to me after my father raised a bit of hell informing the head Master and the psychiatrist that they were both idiot Americans, and much much more—or so I believe. Got to love ignorance in people.

After I left the US Army in 2000, yes I served in two armies. It's great, and even I sometimes get confused, which uniform to wear, which way to salute, which way to march. Oh I'm surprised I lived through it. I ended up having another problem though added on to my CV of disabilities due to my military service. I received a disorder called PTSD, or Post Traumatic Stress Disorder. I can't go into why I got it because it pains me too much to talk about it. I can say that being diagnosed with it has made my life even harder for me to contend with. However it is better to be diagnosed then to wonder what is wrong with me. Everyday I have to take a pill that keeps my brain in order, but if I miss one pill, oh boy, watch out sheep here comes daddy. But at least her Majesty awarded me for my effort of doing my job in the tough world we live in.

Stepping back a bit however before the military while living in Seattle, Washington during high school I had the chance to join a high school band which again I thought was a great, this time my luck was working for me. Shorecrest High School, had the only pipe band in Washington State at that time which was great for me.

Some of my friends or who I always thought were my friends joined up as well, because wearing a kilt, well you guys know what it does for a growing boy with hormones! We had fun though running around the Pacific Northwest wearing a kilt and flirting with the girls. I went everywhere with that school's band. But after two years my parents were on the move again, this time for the east coast. Our family moved to New England, which at first I thought was terrible, because Seattle is a great place, but now today, I miss the atmosphere, weather and the small villages of New England. The school I went too was an old military school during the Victorian age called Norwich Free Academy, but now is a private school. But even here I still went back and forth to England and Scotland to play the pipes winning many piping competitions for my age group of under 16.

When I was done with school I had many choices given to me. Join the military, work at Burger King, or go professional with the pipes. Well I didn't know how to go professional on the bagpipes, my disabilities sometimes cause me to question myself. I saw how the military had caused out family to move around the world and cause him problems, not even working in his own country for that matter. Well Burger King, I did it but not long. I worked small jobs here and there, but always doing my best at them. With my family moving around so much, I ended up travel a lot at this time. I felt like I was a business man, part time in the US, part time in the UK and with family in the UK that worked for the government and family in the US that worked for the government I was spending a lot of time traveling to see both family and friends in the governments, allowing me also to travel to other parts of the world as well. Which I took full advantage of and saw every continent and many wonders.

There was a moment back when I was in my 20's that then I thought was a bit cheeky but now today I think was great. It was after the Black Watch Pipe Band was doing a tour in the US and they came by Seattle on the tour. I went down to see a few of the pipers who were friends a long time ago and I dressed up in my kilt and kit, sat and watched the performance which I remember of course was being grand and wonderful as only the Black Watch could do.

As the performance broke up I left walking down the hallway inside the stadium looking at some vendors who were selling trinkets when a group of young boys ran up to me and asked me if I was with the band. Well I wasn't of course but before I could say anything they all screamed like I was a rock star or something asking for my signature on the band LP album that they had just bought. Their adult escort that was with them just smiled and gave me the 'ok' look so I signed the album asking them what they were hoping to do with their lives. Most said that they wanted to learn to play the pipes and have fun doing it. A few said that they were looking forward to joining the army or being famous sport stars. It was a great time for me and I remember it now as chance to hopefully show a young child that they could do everything. Hey everyone has that moment that was mine to be a rock star!

So enough of me talking about boring things like my life. Now let me share some of the many stories that I have retained in my short memory.

MEMORABLE

My piping career started taking off when I was around 13 or so, at least that is the point that I thought it was. Even before that though I played for many important people on many continents, but of course the best and most memorable time for me in my career was playing for her Majesty the Queen when I was 10 years old. A cousin of my father's, Paul Channon, who at that time was Margaret Thatcher's Secretary of Transportation, informed my grandfather that the queen was near us at Balmoral while we were on holiday fishing. He thought it would be nice if this young boy (me) who played the bagpipes would come and give the queen a wee bit concert since her normal piper has gotten sick and was unable to play his morning serenade. Of course I wasn't told who I was going to play for at the time as I was rushed into my wee kilt and got out my wee bagpipes then just told to have fun. I showed up in my wee uniform. I must have looked so cute. I was given some quick lessons on the proper way to walk in, where to stand and where to play, and even on how to talk if talked too, though I still didn't know who I was to play for. All this excitement was making me a bit nervous, but I walked and played through my performance without a hitch, and once I was done I bowed and finely got a good look. Oh shit! Is that who I think it is. I really hoped that she didn't know much about piping! Of course that was false hope, however I was told she had a good time with no complaints. It's good to be the Queen!

Yet another family member who gave me an experience of a life time however this one had nothing to with the bagpipes but it was memorial none the less. He played football (soccer in the US) for England, specifically for Southampton but some of the other big teams in England as well. Michael 'Mick' Channon, gave me the chance to try out for the under 15's team. Of course I did try, hoping that at least I could play in the goal keeper's position, my strongest position, however I did not make the team. At least I can always say I tried, even though I didn't make it mainly because I kept missing the ball when it was shot at me. I kept tripping or falling into the poles, once getting tangled up in the net, to much pressure. Which usually for me pressure is easy to overcome but I am much older now. I still had a good time though, and what an experience. My cousin is such great guy, one of the best people I've always thought, someone to look up too as well. Now Michael is training horses all over Britain and having a great time at it.

When I met my wife, she had just graduated that year with a degree in marketing and management, and knew how to get my image and music out into the music and wedding market. Right off the bat her marketing knowledge encouraged requests from local schools and hospitals to participate in their auctions to raise funds for their kids, which I was more than happy to do as I am also a teacher of history and love helping kids. Within the first few weeks of her contacting some organizers in Seattle I had a few auctions to play for including a private school in south Seattle. Now this auction was huge and had everything; food, jewelry, and huge amounts of cash rolling around. I was asked to walk around in my uniform and just talk to people. I'm really good at that, so that's what I did. For an hour I walked around with my soon to be wife and we looked at auction items, talked with people and had appetizers. When it came down to do the auctioneering time, I went outside to hide. The auctioneer was a friend of my wife's and she and I had made arrangements that I was to walk in playing the pipes through the audience, then up on to the catwalk, playing and strutting my stuff. I did my best to get my pipes warmed up with out anyone hearing, then ready or not I came back in when told. Consequently after about 20-30 minutes my time came and I walked in and up the stairs and started to play up and down the catwalk. The tune I chose was something everyone knew, 'Scotland the Brave'. It's interesting to note, that you never know how many people are in a place until you get up above them, looking down at people from a catwalk is a whole new experience. It's kind of awing in away. I played and just had fun walking up and down the catwalk slowly strutting my stuff. When I went down off the stage well then the fun really started. Yes during these auctions, I was sold, yes sold well actually it was my piping service however the way it was presented, well you understand. I had to walk the catwalk and get bought by someone. Of course this was done in my kilt and playing the pipes which the girls do love as I swing my hips. I do love the reactions I get from girls when in my kilt, well the accent doesn't hurt either. My wife tells me that is how I got her attention. The single and even married women in the crowd were going crazy and I felt like I was in the rock concert again. That is another story. The hands went up and the money rolled out for me. It is a good thing my wife is not a jealous person. I don't really remember what I ended up getting for the school but I know it was in the high hundreds of dollars. I ended up being auctioned off to a lady who asked me to play for her daughter's birthday party coming up, which I had a great time at. When I went down off the stage well then the fun really started for other ladies, that I didn't even notice before, just came up and talked my ears off asking me tons of questions, "Where are you from?" "What's underneath the kilt?" "Are you married?" It was a blast, so much fun!

The next auction for a school was again a private school. This time ladies somehow knew I was going to be there, I think it was a small community for there were some similar faces. My ears were talked off yet again as a lot of them were the same ladies that had been at the previous auction. So here I was being given drinks and flirting with, which I liked, ha ha. It was then that I discovered how understanding my wife is when I'm being flirted with, there was no jealousy coming from her mind. She just stood back and watch, I think she enjoyed it as well. Of course the questions were flying yet again, with the most common being, "Are you married?" In the end at this auction I ended up being auctioned off to a gentlemen who was having a party for his wife in a few weeks and he though it would be fun for me to play for her. He was a big and important man in the construction business in the area so people knew he had money. When the party came around, my fiancée and I drove over to their place. Their house was just huge and on a private lake in south Seattle. The interesting thing I thought was that their house was also decked out like it was the 60's again, plush carpet on the walls, and orange too. The alcohol was flowing everywhere and this guy had a whirlpool going with both kids and girls in bikinis coming in and out, I thought I was at the playboy mansion for a second there. I only played for about five minutes according to his request but his wife loved it. I heard that a few years later he died of cancer which was too bad, he was such a great guy to know too.

The next catwalk I was asked to participate in was for an annual bridal show that goes on in Seattle. The management of the show thought it was going to be fun for me to play as the show highlighted some of the newest Scottish wedding dresses that one of the designers had made up. What made it really fun for me was making jokes of the girls that walked the catwalk before me swinging their hips as I played and me wearing a kilt I fit right in and all those girls loved it. I was asked to sit in the back of the stage and wait until it was time for me to play. The plan was for me to walk out and down the catwalk playing as the girls walked around me showing the dresses. The fun part for me being a guy was waiting in the back I got my first glance at what a designer dress show was like, girls running around, changing, walking up and down the stage, then changing again. You'd think I would be uncomfortable sitting there watching these girls changing, I'm not a voyeur believe me, but they just did it in front of me. I saw everything, and I mean everything. What a dream job, it's good to be the bagpiper.

Another auction I ended up getting bought by this young lady. And sitting next to her for the rest of the dinner, oh boy, the thoughts because she was a looker! It's a good thing I have an understanding wife. She just happened to know some people that might want to have a bagpiper play for either a party or event. One of them was this gentleman named Scott Oki, who was a retired Microsoft CEO and was building a golf course on a large hill east of Seattle. This hill was in the past was a dumping ground and he was going to make it into Seattle's premier golf course. I learned later it had a terrible odor during the summer, you just can't get rid of the junk that sinks into the ground and the smell, oh it was terrible sometimes but the view of the city was fabulous. Anyway, he wanted to have a bagpiper come out and play for him and his guests every night at sunset, once the golf club opened, just like what he saw on television recently when the golfer Paine Stewart passed away. Stewart was a popular golfer, at his funeral they had a bagpiper play on the golf course to celebrate his Scottish ancestry. So starting that summer, I ended up opening the Golf Course at Newcastle playing for over 5 years, leaving in 2004 to continue my studies in education at a university in the UK. But the time that I was there, oh the fun, made a lot of friends and contacts, it was so worth it.

I remember the 4th of July each year, I would get done playing on my wee hill just to time to watch the fireworks start up behind me around the city of Seattle. It was fantastic to watch, it was like wee bit explosions around the city. People from all over the city would come up to the course to hear me and watch the fireworks. The popularity that I was giving this place was fantastic and they loved it plus I was able to meet people from all over the world.

While playing at the Golf club, one night I was asked to play for Bill Gates one of the owners and CEO of Microsoft at a dinner which was another memorable time for me. Here was the most important person or rather one of the richest people in the world and I was getting the chance to play for him. It was incredible. The only thing was of course I wouldn't get the chance to speak with him, which was ok as I had to blow my pipes which meant my mouth was a wee bit preoccupied making it hard to speak anyway. I might have spat on him. After I played I was standing next to Mr. Gates talking to some gentlemen. I actually did not know how close Mr Gates was to me at the time. I was holding my pipes on my shoulder when someone called my name. When I turned my bass drone hit Mr. Gates in the face, no damage but how embarrassing. Mr. Gates even laughed about it making a joke or two. I'm such a nut.

The rest of the dinner went well except I did play the wrong tune, which believe it or not happens from time to time! No one noticed or said anything which was good. I didn't think they would really notice because they really just wanted to hear a tune or two, it had just been a suggestion from the person hosting the dinner.

Playing the wrong tune happened one other time. While playing for the military retirement dinner. I was to play some type of Irish tune because the commander was Irish. It did not matter which one however as I started to play for some reason my disabilities kicked in and I started to play "Danny Boy". One which is really not one to play for someone when they are leaving a battalion or just retirement, really. Because it's more of an Irish funeral tune, really not the most excellent tune at a time of celebration. However it was still a hit and enjoyed by all.

I've even had the chance to play the bagpipes in a rock band when I was much younger. Yes in a rock band. Something I can check off my bucket list of things to say I've done. Well there is actually not much left on that list but one just has to find new things to add. Though playing in the band, and PLAYING IN THE BAND for me were two different things. Playing the pipes for heavy metal, well only AC/DC had done it up to then, so it was new to me, but man it was fun. But the one and only performance I gave was at a school concert which ended up with me on the front page of the paper, not because of my playing or the band, which was called 'Shattered'. No, it was because my car was broken into that night sitting in the car park and was then used as a base of operations for selling drugs to kids coming to our concert. I was arrested then released later however I was shown in the newspaper picture holding the moonlight glass of my car yelling at a police officer with the look like, what the hell dude?

I love drunks at weddings, parties and such they are a blast to watch. My wife calls it people watching, something she showed me later while we sat in a mall just watching people as they walked by. Seeing the best man go up to do his speech and fall over while he was talking, or the maid of honor throwing up on the bride, these are memories I will always have, though many I wish I didn't. I have so many of types of memories form the many weddings but you got to love the one memory when I was dancing with someone, and was asked to dance by a guy that came up behind me. He was drunk and thought I was a girl. Then there was the once I saw a bride making out with the best man a wedding because she was drunk, you think the ended the marriage fast, well that marriage end but the affair kept going and going. One wedding, I heard that the caterer hit on the bride because he even got drunk, making her slap him. I won't say who's, oh wait that was mine. My wife didn't tell me for a few years fearing that I might go kill the caterer which happened to be a friend at the time. I think I would if I had know at the time, don't you?

I can't remember how old I was when this story took place I think I was about 18 maybe 20 years old and I was living in London at the time. London unlike say L.A., but like New York City its very easy for a person that is famous to get lost in the crowds. One day while up at Hyde Park just standing there practicing like I always did near the Peter Pan statue, which by the way is one of my favorite stories of all time. I was playing for maybe 10-15 minutes not paying any attention to the people that stopped and took pictures, or the animals that came by when I turned around and saw a gentlemen standing off to the side taking a picture with a lovely looking girl standing near by. I nodded but kept playing turning around like I do or making a small circle to keep time in my head. When I came around a few moments later he was still there, he waved like he wanted to talk to me so I stopped playing as best I could. It was during that last moment that of course if done wrong the pipes really do make their famous dead cat sound, and yep mine did. I smiled and walked over joking that they just hadn't had their pint today and were a wee bit mad at me.

Of course while my pipes were draining away I took more notice of the gentleman in front of me and knew who it was right off. Even though I'm terrible with names, I'm great with faces. I can remember meeting or seeing someone and years later remember then again. I walked up and shook his hand and he introduced himself and the young lady with him. He along with the young lady were in London doing some shopping while he was doing some work up in north London. I was keeping calm but how can you, here's Michael Caine talking to me, my favorite actor of all time really talking to me like I was a normal guy. In the end, we talked more about what I was doing and that he loved the music I was making and thought where I was was

23

just perfect, with the back ground of the water and the statue. He asked for my picture which I thought waht an honor, right off and we had a good time speaking. My only regret was that I never got a picture of us together myself, I would have loved it. Years later I met him again while in Edinburgh while he was doing a book tour. He remembered me of course but I had my duuuhhh moment and forgot again to get a picture of us. Oh well it will happen someday I think.

Family in Cumbria

Military event in Middle East

Practicing with Father

Family home in Cumbria

with Gary Paden

Family home in cambridgeshire

LEFT, RIGHT LEFT!

The military weddings that I have done over the years, with myself being in both the US and British military, though both enjoyable and very interesting have also been very rigid. Recent years have seen this style of wedding relax more and more. These weddings have gotten even a wee bit over done, I think going to extremes. It seems that the September 11th 2001 attacks in the United States produced a patriotic feeling towards anything military and anything to do with the military has to be at its best. I can understand why. When I started playing so many years ago, military weddings were very plain, very quiet and short. Now days many military weddings are almost like any other wedding that you might see in the civilian world, but with men or women are in uniform, then the extra touches leaning more toward the military look.

Now I am not saying that the military has weird weddings, I mean most military weddings I've seen have had a small amount of guests with very few to no extras in the church such as no flowers or music. A few times I was even ordered not to play in the church at all, by ministers mostly. So in a way military weddings are in some of the best I've been in because like the military they are carried off with almost perfectly precision. Now I say almost because not even the military is perfect for sometimes even they can mess up. After that terrible day in America, September 11th and the fact that military weddings seemed to have changed I now have seen military weddings that have guns going off, go-fast boats shooting by, even a plane going over a few times. Later I'll tell you of one that I was in that had something like a James Bond experience in it, but that's later.

My first military wedding was when I was 10 years old. I was with my father at one of his churches at the time when the husband to be came over and asked my father about some ideas or rather help with the plans for their wedding. My father was a church organist as he still is today and was going to play for their wedding, so in many ways I had an in. I heard the groom ask about a bagpiper saying that he found one, but the gentleman was never able to make any meetings or return phone calls. My father then mentioned that I was a piper, though young and not with much experience I might be able to play. The groom came over to me and we talked a while and in the end I was hired to play for the ceremony. It was entertaining seeing all the uniforms and such walking around during the wedding, with myself only in a dress shirt and tie with my kilt. Though at that time my kilt was just a regular base tartan, nothing special, today I wear my own clan which is Clan Donald, or Clan MacDonald, though I do have a Hunting Stewart and a Clan Douglas as well. The day of the wedding I was to walk the groom's father in, and then walk the groom in at the beginning of the ceremony. In a British military wedding traditionally the uniforms and the method things are done are very formal and some what refined, especially when it comes to weddings. Things like the ritual at this ceremony of having the bride and groom be escorted out by a piper under an archway of swords drawn and held up, usually by the groomsman or chosen companions. One British tradition that many militaries took over as the centuries progressed. So after walking the groom in, and then the bride came up, I learned from the very beginning to stand off to one side, usually behind the groomsmen, however more than once on the side of the bridesmaids. I make the joke now saying that since I'm wearing a kilt which is a lot like a dress no one would mistake me for anyone except a bridesmaid anyway. This wedding went off with out any predicament or unusually activity. My father played the organ and I piped the couple out after the ceremony while men in uniform drew swords high overhead, trying to make sure they didn't cut me or at the very least they had to leave my pipes undisturbed. Even though I was small at the time, my pipes weren't, and every once in a while I hit on one of their swords, causing me to waver on the tune. This also caused some marks on my bass pipe drone even to this day. Since this was my first military event and the fact that things went so smoothly, this led me to many others.

The next military wedding that comes to mind was a

religious wedding with a military flare to it. The groom was in the US Army while the bride was some assistant to some assistant in the government, the FBI is the last I heard. They had met while working in Washington D.C., which I have heard is a good place for military people to meet and get attached as they all gather there to work and play. I've always called it the Imperial City because of the power that is stationed there, just like Rome.

Anyway, so they called me up and ask me to meet them. We met on a warm day at a park on the east side of Lake Washington near the suburb of Bellevue, near where I was living at the time. You know the term, first impressions are the best or worst, well when I first saw them I thought, what the hell, this guy looks like he can pick up a car not only with his arms, but his head! His neck was as big as his legs and man was she a looker, not only in the beautiful way either but in the fact that she was so petite. They were an odd couple, looking like David and Goliath in a way but because I was brought to never say anything bad in regards to someone, I was polite and talked with them. They turned out to be a wonderful couple. They wanted me to play for her walking in mainly the basic stuff in the end. Walk in, walk out, and play in the middle of the ceremony. It turned out that even though he was in the army, and some of the people in the wedding were as well, however since it was going to be in a catholic church in Seattle there wouldn't be a lot of military fluff.

Don't get me wrong I don't mind the Catholic Church, my wife is a Catholic, but I can't stand organized religion.

It's got some good things going for itself, but man the ceremonies catholics have are the worst, long and drawn out. Especially this one at the end of the day this wedding was over three hours. I was only paid to walk the bride in, play in the middle and walk them out but not sitting in the loft for over three hours. I was in misery by the time the end of the wedding came. Not because of boredom, no I learned a long time ago from my father to bring something like a book or magazine, nothing that would make too much noise, of course. I knew one piper in England that brought his walkman and played it during long weddings like this one. The only problem with that was he played it too loud one day, and was kicked out of the church by a priest until the wedding was over. Bad mistake mate! If you want to do that, just TURN IT DOWN!!! Back to this ceremony, as my luck would have it that day turned out to be one of the hottest on record until that time in Seattle, and knowing churches like I do, they don't have air conditioning or much ventilation. So standing up there in the loft sweating my life away in my kilt, which included eight yards of wool wrapped around me. Another thing that was added to this ceremony before I got there was that all the seats in the loft where being painted, not allowing me to sit at all during this three hours. What a time to paint them I thought. Oh did I tell you I was allergic to wool. Yes ever since I was a kid I couldn't wear wool unless the weather was really cold, like it is in Scotland. Only when it is below say under 15 degrees celsius could I really wear my kilt comfortably. Here I was in over 90 degree fahrenheit weather in Seattle wearing a wool kilt with a formal wool jacket, high in the rafters of a church with no air conditioning and not able to sit down. I was dying for three hours! I still think I lost 20 pounds of water that day just sweating it off. When it was over, my only relief was getting outside to the wee bit cooler air. Even with the long obligation of dying in the rafters the bride and groom were very beautiful and the wedding went well. However the most hurtful part of this ceremony was that the wedding couple didn't even in the end give me any thanks, or offer me a tip. Something I knew I might have to add something into my contract sometime soon about the length of time for a wedding as I have never charged for the time period just the things that I do during the wedding. I still charge that way today. My basic look at life is if your nice to me and we get along, I'll probably let things go. Oh well. From what I had heard, the couple is living very well in California, he got out of the army as a Captain and is now working for a computer manufacture in Los Angeles or near there and she works near Hollywood.

One of the funniest military weddings I've done in a long time was this one I thought was right out of "Three Weddings and a Funeral". The groom wore his family's kilt with his US Marines uniform on top. He had it made so that the two wouldn't look weird together and received special permission for the variance to his uniform. This was years before the Marines came out with their own tartan. His bride to be was also a Marine. When I saw her I thought that she could take on the whole Iraqi army even a politician or two. Great girl, still friends with her even to this day, but man was she buff. When this couple called to inquire about my services, I was working with another couple at the time that wanted to have an off the wall wedding using animals, I'll tell you later about that one, and for some reason my humor just came out at the time. They took it in stride and hired me on the spot. When we finally did meet, we met at a pub which for me is not the best place to meet, because when the beer starts to flow, then things start to go wrong. As my wife likes to constantly remind me I am a light weight when it comes to drinking beer. We met and ordered drinks and things went nuts after twenty minutes or so. They wanted to have a military wedding, but not a modern one. I was intrigued now so I asked, "What type of military wedding are you thinking?" I'm a knowledgeable person when it comes to different military customs and traditions from around the world so I wanted to know. They both wanted to have a wedding from the early 18th century American by dressing up as English soldiers and people during that time period. I thought great I love that time period in history this will be a great wedding.

We sat and planned for about four hours where I believe we went over every aspect of the wedding, from music, to the dresses and uniforms, to themselves. I became good friends with them that night and we started doing things besides talking about the wedding. My father always said not to get to close to clients, but these guys were very nice and cool to hang out with. Actually in later years many of my best friends are people that I was involved in their wedding. When you get invited to the bachelor party then you know things are really looking good for you, as far as friendships go. About five or so weeks before the wedding the groom asked me to come over with him and meet some friends. I followed him in my car and we got to his place, which was a small house in northern Seattle. We walked in and there were girls, guys and beer everywhere. It was great! And being single at the time, I was looking for a certain friend to meet. That part of this story is for another time but I'll tell you that we all had a great time that night, even to the point that I ended up staying over because I was too drunk. I've never done that before and never did it again. I'm still a professional but at that time I was young, so give me a break please.

That week I went out with the bride to review the wedding location, where we talked more about what I would do. I had many ideas to add on as final suggestions. The area that they were doing the wedding was an open ground with some trees making a sort of arch way for a table and ceremony. The ceremony itself would be simple and elegant in an 18th century style with the groom and his men in the uniform of the time, while she chooses to wear a simple 18th century dress which included a full bussel. At first we thought of having me play at the front because she wanted everyone to be looking at me and the groom. Then because of the sun location at the time of the ceremony, we figured out that the crowd would staring right into it. We decided to move the wedding around a wee bit so the sun would hit the side of the audience and not full force in the face. Then I would come walking out from behind some trees about 20 meters away playing the pipes and behind me would be the bride. She wanted at first to come in on a boat but because the boat launch was a wee bit away, and the dress she decided to wear came into play so that was limited out. I find it amazing some of the ideas that people want to include in a wedding, unfortunately so many are limited out because of time and just logistics. This is too bad because of a lot of them are interesting. It is only in the movies that things like a boat ride down the river in a long white gown don't go very wrong. This is where it really got interesting for this ceremony for we planned the wedding like this, I would start playing behind a couple of trees where the audience wouldn't see me. I would play for about a minute, and then stop, wait for a minute or two, and then start up again. All this would be started by a signal; at first it was just going to be a wave of the hand from one of the groomsman, then from the father of the groom, then the priest, then..... Finally it came to a certain guest in the crowd. I'm standing there waiting with the bride, and then a fire truck drove by with its alarms on. That made it a wee bit weird, however the problem was, it drove by when the signal was given so I didn't see it or even hear it. Here was this guy, one of the spectators, waving up and down like a bird trying to get my attention. When I did see him, I started to play. I'm playing for about 30 to 40 seconds, when a fireman ran out of the trees and asked me to stop. "No problem", thinking that something must be wrong, why would a fireman ask me to stop. He ran away, but then came back and said "OK, you can play now, but keep it down; we are trying to stop a fire next door here". I'm standing there looking at the bride when he said this, "Ok to play, but keep it down?" I'm thinking in my head, "Ok, yea sure mate, I can do that....yea right!!!" I tried to play, standing near a tree, thinking that it might keep it down. Meanwhile the fire next door had cause a large amount of smoke and that smoke had started to cross the field that the guests were sitting in, and some were getting sick. The bride didn't know, the priest didn't know and I sure didn't, I'm keeping myself hidden and trying to be quiet when I'm playing. The priest walks out, sees the smoke and runs back to ask the bride what to do. She is going nuts by this point and looks at me; giving me the "Walk" nod so off I go, starting to walk out. So while this huge fire is going on about 100 meters from us, the bride, groom and myself plus the guests are having a wonderful time at this smoky but elegant wedding. Then you never really think about it, but now it was pretty funny. I never did find out why that fireman asked me to stop playing, and then only play softly however I did find out that no one was hurt in the fire; it was an abandoned house, so there were no worries. The couple asked everyone at the wedding afterwards to go with them to the reception, which was at a small boat club down on the water. When we got there, the groom really thought he was seeing things for we got there smoke was coming out of the boat. He then asked me to make sure that the smoke coming out the ship wasn't another fire. I ran in and made sure, it was just a smoky piece of fish I found out. This made for an interesting reception, very fishy. For the next two weeks I heard that the bride had feelings that there was a fire everywhere she went. Interesting, I'd hate to have that feeling myself.

After this, I thought no other military wedding could beat that one. I was wrong. The next one that comes to mind was at Fort Knox, Kentucky where I was living for a while during the late 90's. I was asked by a major in the armored corps of the army to play for his bride to be and himself. I was more than happy too. What he wanted was everyone to be played in at the beginning, bridesmaids, groomsman, family and all. This is a pretty normal thing to see at weddings, except this. The groom was going to wear his uniform which of course was normal for the military, but the bride was going to wear her bridal dress over a black tight suit. No one was told of this except for certain people, and I ended up being one of those. Why, no idea at the time. I was to play songs such as "Scots Wha Hea", and "Scotland the Brave", because the groom always thought Scotland the Brave was the national anthem of Scotland. At that time it wasn't, still isn't and have no idea when Scotland will ever come up with a real official national anthem, but who am I to disagree with the groom. The groom wanted me to wear the uniform of a British officer. I didn't think that was right, so I fought it a wee bit. The bride ended up giving me a wee bit more money for it, however the uniform was not much different then my British uniform from years earlier so I wore that one. I didn't think I could have gotten in trouble for that. So wearing a sword, something British officers normally don't wear, but the groom wanted it. For your information, try not to wear things that can hurt you or others if you're not used to wearing them. During the reception I ended up hitting someone with that sword when my name was called, I turned around, and "WHAM!" A sword in the crotch! Ouch, that must have hurt, and he wasn't laughing. Anyway, so I'm wearing a sword, and a dirk, a wee knife in the sock, I felt that if the army wanted me back I was ready. I would have gone anywhere and fought anyone for I was armed to the teeth and playing the bagpipes. Well, I knew I could scare anyone really well. I was to stand off to one side and play one of these songs as the groom, and his four groomsmen walked by me. This is what I was told, and this was what we had practiced. Right at the last minute, and I mean at the last minute, they decided to include another officer from the army that was to play the trumpet right before me. I stood inside the church waiting for this guy to finish, waiting, waiting, and waiting. Nothing, this guy loved to play, not that I was complaining about his playing, it was great to hear the trumpet being played right but he didn't stop. Then the groomsmen came in, but the trumpet player was still going. Then the groom came in himself and looked at me and gave me that look, "Hey, why aren't you playing?" I gave that look, "Trumpet!" He nodded his head, but kept going. I ended up not playing at all during that first part of the wedding. Then the brides came in. This is where it got really interesting. The bride walked in, gave me that look like the groom, "Why aren't you playing", I gave her the same nod. She then turned around and walked outside, with the trumpet still sounding. Then we hear a loud, "Ow that hurts!" The bride had hit someone. I am not sure if it was on purpose or by accident but it caused the trumpeter to stop, she quickly walked back in, so I started to play. No problem, I did what I was supposed to do. During the wedding another person came and played another instrument. This was great, so many different instruments, but again this person thought they had the whole show for themselves, and the bride had to walk over and shut them up as well. Oh well, it was great show and led to some interesting conversations afterwards. I walked the couple out playing, and saw the trumpet player outside still rubbing his stomach with a mean look on his face. At that time I confirmed that it was him she hit. At the reception he again played for a long time, this time asking me if I wanted to join in. We tried playing together however I kept overpowering him especially with both instruments next to each other. Who do you think would win? Me! No one could really hear him, so I walked off to the corner. You really can't turn down the Highland Pipes. I've been asked at another wedding later to do the same, trying to play with a French horn, but that didn't work either. The pipes are just too loud! However, through all this the only thing actually military in this wedding was that the groom wore his uniform.

The next event I did with the military wasn't a wedding but a promotion party for the Navy. This was fun because I'd never done anything with the navy before, other then making fun of my wife, who served in the Navy. My fear of that vast ocean with all its sharks always kept me from joining the Navy. That's why I was in the army. If the ship sinks you can only go so far, however if in the army if one needs to get away from that one spot or the need to run arises, I have vast amounts of space around me to run to! The promotion party was pretty simple. I wasn't going to play at the ceremony, but at the after party. I arrived at the base just west of Seattle and sat in my car while the promotion ceremony went on. When everyone walked out, I then played the guests to the building where the reception was to be held. The weather was great, but only one problem. The building was near the airstrip. That moment that I started playing a jet flew over, then one took off, loud was putting it mildly. It even beat out my pipes which is hard to do, however I continued to play. What was to be a three minutes performance on my part turned into a one minute rush of jet fumes as all the fighter jets flew over head. The newly appointed Captain came up to me and gave me a good tip and asked me in to the reception. I sat off to the side and was proceeded to get attacked by navy wives. What a life! They just loved the kilt, it was a good thing I was married by this time. It kept me out of some major problems.

THE NAME IS BOND, JAMES BOND

Another military wedding that I did was for a friend that was in the army. I guess I should clarify, it was the British army. He had joined the paratroopers or "Paras" during the early 1980's, and did a lot of things with them even in his first year before actually assigned to the Paras. Well of course like most guys in the army he met a young girl on his first posting. They fell in love and had the shortest engagement I had heard of at the time, which was only three days. With only three days to prepare he found away to make their wedding perfect and one to remember. Of course one of the first things the groom did was ask me to play, but then he and two of his mates, who were both in the army, had a special touch to add to the ceremony. I was only 13 at the time, he was 17. His younger brother and I were mates so that's how we met. Anyway, this wedding was going to be in the village, he asked me not to say which one, (southwest of London). I played the bride in at the beginning of the ceremony and the groom would come in an abnormal but incredible way. I was not even told at the time what that would be. As far as I can remember, the groom's friend had a thing for James

Bond. He always thought he would be a great Bond whenever Roger Moore retired. Anyway, after seeing a film where Bond parachutes out on a mission, he wanted to do just that. The military regulations however were against this type of action especially in populated areas. At least that was my understanding, but I was never able to verify it. Hence here I am walking the bride down the street into the church when I and everyone else hear a plane going over head, I am able to quickly look up and see three people parachute out. Everyone including myself thought, oh cool, that's neat, but what a place to do that. I stood there playing the pipes while everyone was looking to the sky. At first, like everyone there, I wondered what are they doing and who they were. However as they got closer, I noticed that they were wearing tuxedos. They were the groom and the groomsman. My next thought was at least they weren't wearing kilts! They landed and some guy that no one noticed but me ran out and collected the chutes, then helped the groom and his jolly men out of their fittings. He ran over to the bride and then I saw something I'll never forget. You think it would have been all happy and joyous stuff. No, the bride slapped the groom across the face so hard, he fell over. She walked into the church in a huff, the groom just laid on the ground for a moment. He explained she's just nervous or something. I heard later that she was so mad, she almost cancelled the wedding. What a day!

I was asked once to play the bagpipes at a local Irish pub for St. Patrick's Day in Portland, Oregon. I've done many of these over the years in Ireland, New England, and even in China. I lived in Seattle at the time and my wife's family lived near the pub, so we decided it could be a family event. My wife's cousin was the bartender at this pub that called itself the best Irish pub in Portland due to its inventory of beers on tap, claiming to have more than any other in the area. The owner of the place was a little old lady who ran it like a Gestapo camp— everything was done to her specification; if you didn't like it, you were out. This owner rang me up a while before Patty's Day and asked if I could play between the three bands who were playing that night. Actually, the whole day of festivities was to start at noon. No problem; I thought, I could do that. So while each band was breaking down and setting up, I stood off to the side and played a long list of Irish and Scottish tunes that would go well for Paddy's Day. She also asked if I could give her a Bio and a picture so she could advertise me in the local Portland paper. My wife took care of both for me; I trust her. When we arrived in Portland around 10 a.m., we headed straight for the pub. As we walked in, of course the place was dead. A local rock radio station was setting up in the corner and one of the bands was practicing so my wife and I sat in the corner and had a drink to warm up. The owner came over and we went over the schedule of the night. Turns out that she wanted me to play more than what we had spoken about on the phone but being the nice guy, I had no problem with this for my wife said that she had arranged for me to be paid by the hour. As it also turned out, the photo my wife sent was me in my kilt with this nerdy smile on it. Oh so Embarrassing!

Around 1:00 p.m., I started playing before each band came on however only for a few minutes for there were only a few people in the place. Each band would play for about twenty minutes, so I had time in between. By the time 9 p.m. came around, I had been on at least twenty or more times. I lost count and I was getting tired. Originally what started as playing only about four times was now tons of times; however, I was good spirit about it. The crowd started getting larger as the day wore on and of course the beer was flowing. At around 9:00 p.m., the place was packed and my wife asked me to get us drinks at the bar, which was an adventure in itself because of the crowds. From the stage, you get a different look; for it was fun watching all the drunks singing along with the bands and myself. However, when I was in the crowd it became another adventure altogether; everywhere I walked whether up to the stage, to the bar, or even to the restroom, I was felt up by every single woman in the place. These were not little or simple pinches either. My willie, arse, and other things were all grabbed by each woman and I couldn't do a thing about it because of the small amount of room to maneuver. Oh well, if I was single I might have had more fun with this until I saw the girls who were doing the feeling. Now I know how Bond feels sometimes. My wife got a kick out of it, so at least someone got some enjoyment.

THE ANIMAL STORIES

When it comes to animals being included in weddings, I've always loved it however it is a bit of a challenge for animals are always unpredictable. I'm a huge animal lover; my dogs over the years have always received the best love that I can offer them for they are a part of my family. So when one wedding couple asked me to play for them while the bride would ride a white horse, I was thrilled. This being my first wedding involving an animal I did not know what was in store. I soon found out this was not to be the only animal involved in this ceremony. The couple were members of a group known as SCA, or the Society of Creative Anachronism and I would be entertaining the guests as they arrived. Standing off to the side and at the end of the wedding walkway, I was to play while the groom walked the bride in on the horse towards the altar, then play when they walked out. However, nothing is as simple as it seems for this is what happened. The bride and groom walked out with the white horse following, I started playing and the horse who had obviously never heard bagpipes, fricked out by rearing up and getting out of control so at this point I stopped playing. Lucky the bride was not on her yet.

Everyone attending this ceremony was dressed up as 12th century English and Scottish lords and ladies, including the wedding party with one gentleman dressed as the king. The bride had chosen to wear flowers in her hair and an off white dress while the groom was dressed up in all white uniform with gold trim. I thought this was a nice touch but must have been expensive to do. This wedding was to include two doves which were to be released at the end of the ceremony, people dressed like soldiers with halberds (a type of spear), a trio of musicians playing the recorder and violin and hand harp. Yet another escapade to the ceremony was the addition of two Irish wolf hounds who were to serve as part of the wedding party, however these two did not get along with the horse. So everyone had to make sure that these animals were kept apart. When I originally started to play and the horse reacted, it also caused these two dogs to go crazy as well, barking and running off into the forest that was around us. It created even more confusion. A few people from the wedding party ended up chasing after them. It was so entertaining for people that had come to share in the couple's joyful day. Imagine watching these people chasing after one of the second fastest dogs in the world. It was a kick and caused much laughter because one of these people chasing them fell into some mud, getting so messed up he ended up screaming at anyone who came over to help, like something out of an old vaudeville show. However, this is not the end of the story for the dogs ran by the bird cages and ended up somehow releasing the birds. What a surprise and this all happened before the bride even came down the isle. Nevertheless the bride took it all in stride and having grown up with this horse wanted this horse at least to be a part of the ceremony so decided to continue as planned. Trying to ignore everything else I moved off to the side a bit and played once again just a few notes to give the horse a chance to get used to the pipes. The trainer and the groom decided to let the bride get on the horse as I played. Once the bride was on the horse, lucky it did not buck again however it was quite fidgety so instead of riding side saddle with one hand free to greet guests, the bride had to straddle the horse and hold on with both hands, making her dress ride up so everyone could see her knickers. Oops!! It was fascinating and so out of the ordinary to watch all this as I was playing without breaking into a side stitching laughter. The rest of the ceremony went well, however at the end of the wedding the horse still in a fowl mood just decided to bolt away from the wedding party, to be hunted down by the trainer. Now just one more catch to the whole story is that even though the ceremony was over the couple's drinking cups for the reception and their paperwork that had been signed by themselves and the minister was attached to the horse. It was about this time that I had to walk away just laughing, oh, what we do to and for our animals! All in all a very nice wedding however with animals in the ceremony one single person can cause either misery or laughter. After this wedding I have asked any wedding couple to make sure animals that are in their ceremony have heard and react well to bagpipes or other instruments, even offering some practice time with the animals before the ceremony just to be sure. As we all know however animals have their moods and can always be unpredictable so the trick with animals in a ceremony is to remember to be flexible. I have had a few since then and all have been fascinating.

Actually, three weeks later I was asked to do a wedding up in the mountains near the Canadian border, which ended up being one of the hottest days on records up until that time in that area. My luck, I thought! I talked to the couple on the phone for about an hour, speaker phones are so great. This couple were elderly and been married a few times, but they wanted to have their kids in the wedding. Interesting I thought, because a few of them had been fighting over things like who would be the bride's maid and such. Oh families you have to love them! Then they hit me with those words. "We are thinking of having our cat and dog in the wedding as well, basically the whole family." Oh god I thought, is this going to happen again? After some conversation I discovered that the cat was going to be in a cage at least while the dog would be held by a trainer. I informed them of my experiences with animals in weddings, and was a wee bit worried. They understood but really wanted me to play anyway. They were referred by a friend from a party that I had played for a few months earlier, not the animal one but another ceremony. The wedding was in two months, so I didn't need to worry about anything, not even the tunes, as they gave me the choice on what was to be played. So I just played some of my favorite tunes at that time. Over the years this has changed, as in all things do my list of what I consider my favorite tunes has evolved and even expanded, but I always have my traditional favorites, be at "Heiland Laddie", and or "Blue Bonnets". Anyway the day of this wedding is when I found out about the heat. They wanted me in the Prince Charlie tuxedo so I made sure that I had a lot of water both in me readily handy. I arrived like I like to do at least an hour before the weddings or parties and got ready. I brought 3 bottles of water with me, and was through one of them by the time the wedding was getting ready. This one wedding did not have a rehearsal due to a number of reasons including the drive time and location. It was due to be easy, just walk in playing, and leave; nothing hard or special about it. I saw the dog and stood away from him, just in case he decided he did not like the pipes, most dogs like my own like to sing with me, so I hoped the distance between us would help alleviate that. The cat was meowing like the sky was falling. Oh dear! I thought that the dog had been there since I had warmed up, so when I walked over to stand next to the bride, the dog was getting uneasy. I just stood there because I couldn't do a thing. The time came and started up playing and all hell broke loose, really. The dog barked like I was killing his mum, and got away from the trainer, who was by the way the bride's sister. In getting away he hit the cats cage which fell open when it hit the ground letting the cat out, so now the dog and cat were running around. The dog now both chasing the cat, and barking at me, even once getting so close that I jumped on top of a chair. While people were running around trying to get the animals, I sat down next to the bride who was crying a wee bit, and sat there for at least half and hour before they were caught and put away. It amazes me how everyone is so quick to run after animals that get away when usually they return on their own anyway in their own time. Again, what we do to animals!

I have done a number of other weddings where animals have been involved, however not many have been as crazy as the previous two mentioned. Most turn out simple and elegant such as a wedding held at a castle in the local Seattle area, well it looked like a castle, it is more a manor home really. Actually I have had a few couple get married at this location. The owner pretty much is a bitch as she thinks she's the thing. However the house held a beautiful walled garden next to it. This walled garden held a fabulous display of flowers around the outside edge and a path between the wall and the edge of the flowers. At each end of the garden were stairs leading down into the grass area with the pond in the centre. At one end of the garden were stairs that led down to an arch with a bench underneath that stood between two walled towers. I was asked to play while the family and wedding party walked in to the garden area then walk the bride in to the same beautiful garden. The ceremony itself was to be held around the pond, to be more precise on a wooden bridge over the pond. The wooden bridge that was going to be suspended over the water was going to be a great door of old use, with some small legs to go into the water while onlookers gathered around the pond to watch the ceremony. To make this wedding even more unique they were to have two Great Danes as their Maid of Honor and the Best Man and one of these was less than a year old, or as they put it, Dog of Honor and Best Dog. Of the many things one learns from playing the bagpipes is that animals are unpredictable when hearing the pipes for the first time, as I have stated before and no matter how much I warn couples they never seem to listen. Originally the groom was to walk in with the Best Dog and the bride with the Dog of Honor, however after the rehearsal several things changed due to the dog's reaction to the bagpipes. Two handlers were brought in to walk the dogs in ahead of the bride but after the groom, so that by the time I walked in with the bride they were calmer and used to the music. One other thing changed after the rehearsal, the ceremony was not held over the pond. The concept was exceptional but the unsteady nature of the bridge, the edges of the pond were farther apart than was expected, which left too much for chance especially with the Great Danes involved. Instead the ceremony it was held at the end of the garden where the bench and arch stood, which was essential to the uniqueness of this ceremony. Having a wedding at a private home can be unique however make sure you get along with the owner. I've told people in the past to get references from people that have worked with the site before to ensure there were no problems allowing you to ensure what you want to do will be allowed without any problems. For another reason for the changes was due to the owner's reaction to the bridge idea. I hear the bribery works well, use food, flowers, etc. Also remember rehearsals are essential so that you can find out if the plans that you have made will work out with animals involved, specifically reactions to things like music, water and other people.

One story that I would love to tell you about is when I met my dog Troy. It all started back in 2005 when my wife and I were told that we were being kicked out of the flat that had been living in for a few months, the owner missed it and wanted to move back in, go figure. During the last month of living there I started having some medical issues in my right side. Over the next few weeks, I went from just groaning in the middle of the day thinking it was stomach stuff to waking up in the middle of the night screaming in pain. My GP told me what it might be and gave me some medicine but it didn't help. Two days before we were to move out I ended up being taken to the hospital in the middle of the night because the pain was just too much. I had gone from sleeping in the bed with my wife to sleeping in another bed to sleeping on the floor because the cold floor felt good on my stomach. Weird!

It turned out to be a gull bladder problem what normally is the size of a human thumb had blown up to be the size of two thumbs. I knew I was all thumbs but come on. On top of that, it had infected my liver which of course made my eyes and skin turn yellow and made my life hell. I was lucky they said I had maybe 1-2 days and it would have blown up inside of me. I ended up being stuck in the hospital for over 2 weeks as they pumped me with medicines before an after the operation. Of course during this time what hadn't been diagnosed yet was my PTSD, which started to really set in, causing me a lot of issues and I got depressed so bad that another doctor even had to come in and talk to me while I was laid up. Sometime during the first days of being there I must have been under something good because I was sure that the doctor had told me that he saw signs of cancer on my liver as well and that thought bothered me even more! I really was missing the security of having dogs around me.

To make things even worse for me was I was starting back to university to get my masters in history and when this ended I was almost 2 weeks behind the rest of the class so I had lots of catching up to do. My wife while I was in the hospital who didn't tell me until later, ended up moving everything herself and being disabled herself, from a military accident, it was killing her, but she did it!

We moved in to a beautiful 1759 era horse barn that had been turned into 2 flats, we were lucky we got the larger of the two. We both loved living there but with everything going on I was getting more and more depressed making my wife's life even harder and my school work soon suffered. Around a month later my wife finally asked the flat owners if we could get a dog but they said no as the place was historic and they didn't want a dog to damage the place. I understood but even with a psychiatrist saying that a dog would help me the owners kept up a wall against it.

As the months went on my PTSD got dangerous certain thoughts entered my mind all the time, life in beautiful Scotland wasn't what I wanted for my wife to have since leaving the US. She asked and asked about a dog and the owners kept saying no. Now something else was going on at this same time. I had a reaction to the medication they used while in surgery which caused me to just feel like I was itchy all the time.

It was after the Christmas holidays that finally the owner gave my wife permission to walk out of the contract, if we wanted because they could see my depression was worsening and maybe a dog would be the best for me. When my wife told me of this I jumped for joy and began working on what to do. Luck would have it that the same day that I jumped on the internet looking for a dog a local breeder just happened to have one ready to go to a loving family. We ended up moving into a new set of buildings or flats that were being built in the northern area of Edinburgh, in Leith called Western Harbour and we both loved it there. About 2 days of moving in and then we picked up our dog Troy and brought him home.

Right off the bat my wife noticed my depression lighten as Troy took care of me during the day when I was home. His demeanor was one that he knew what was wrong and did his best to lighten up the mood of the house. When I got mad at something or something would bother me he would jump up and give me a look like, 'Its ok daddy I'll take care of you'. Troy has one thing that yes it can be annoying for people but Troy loves to talk to you about his day. Even today when my

PTSD gives me problems Troy is there to make me realize that my life is worth being around. I knew he was the dog for me when I was able to start practicing my pipes finally after recovering, I was nervous that Troy might cause havoc or something. No, he just sat there and cocked his head listening to me play. Suddenly the wee guy just started to howl and was in my ear on key with me. Ever since then Troy comes out and joins me when I'm outside and sings along with me. I love it.

I've never understood why there are people out there that believe that dogs can't help with veterans that use dogs to help with PTSD but I'm a firm believe that it helps. I probably wouldn't be here today if Troy hadn't have helped me. Dogs are smarted than we give them credit for, if you have one give him/her a hug and say thank you everyday, I do!

EASY COME, EASYGO!!

I've found that doing funerals always reminds me of life. It brings you back to reality and makes you remember that you're only human and that life is beautiful even if painful. I've done many funerals over the years; there is only one that made me cry and which I had real trouble playing. Mostly I just don't think about it while I'm there, it's just too hard. Military funerals like their weddings are very formal, but incredibly short. Pretty much here he/she is, yes their dead, let's go party now, bye! Just like the Irish. Living in America the police and fire fighter funerals are the worse, they really get to your heart. They are also full of tradition and are so interesting. Some cultures can take hours when it comes to remembering someone, while others are done within half an hour. So you may find this chapter is a wee bit depressing, but I had to write it as even funerals have funny moments.

A few years ago I was asked to play at a funeral of a gentleman that had passed away from a heart attack. Being a sad event I was more than happy to speak to the widow and family about arranging anything they needed. We got together about two days before the funeral and had tea and talked about the departed, the widow told me about his life. He was an amateur comedian so it was fun to hear about what he did during his life and his adventures. The widow herself was very funny and didn't show any loss at that time in regards to her husband. We got everything worked out, that I was going to play at the church service, then walk out playing of course "Amazing Grace", then get into my car and drive with them to the grave site which was about two or three miles away. There I would play while everyone walked up and paid their respects, and after the service play while they lowered the coffin into the hole. This is where it got a wee bit interesting. I arrived as I normally do at least half and hour before the service, warmed up and then walked around speaking to the minister about anything that might have changed, as things sometimes do. There was just one wee problem, they couldn't find the coffin. The funeral director said that it was supposed to be in the room where they kept coffins, but it wasn't. So people were running around trying to figure out what was going on. What was I supposed to do, nothing, just sit off to the side and wait. About 15 or so minutes after the service was to begin, they found it, someone had delivered it to the grave site instead of the church. Man I would have been upset and mad, but the widow was laughing so hard, she said that her husband would have loved it. The service at the church went well for a funeral anyway, or rather with no problems. They just did it without the coffin there. I got in my car and drove to the grave site and waited for the people to arrive to start playing again.

Which was in about five minutes later and I played for about 10 minutes after people arrived. The minister did the usual speech; family came up and did their speeches. During this time a gentleman came up to me and asked if I had a cigarette. I didn't have one, of course, playing the pipes take all my hot air as it is, so he walked away and drove off. Turns out later that he was boyfriend of the widow, I don't ask. Then I was given the sign so I started playing as the coffin was lowered into the grave. Now hold on here's the really funny part, the coffin was going down into the ground and out of the corner of my eye I saw some smoke coming from the wee bit machine that lowers the coffin. The coffin was about two feet into the grave when the whole thing went nuts. The ropes gave way on one end because the machine holding them broke, the coffin instead of going down tipped over and the body came flying out. That was a new one for me, however I kept playing. I know you are asking yourself how in the world can he have kept playing. It took a lot of work let me tell you. I had to turn around because what made me a wee bit sick was the people around me passing out, some couldn't stop laughing and even some throwing up. I do not do well when others get sick. I think the widow passed out from laughing though. The minister pushed everyone back and signaled for me to keep playing and not stop. Which I did with no problem as long as I looked in another direction, but now I had a problem holding back the giggle that was forming in my throat. Have you ever had that moment when you are trying everything to hold back the laughter and now you are thinking about it and the more you do the harder it becomes. Later I heard this referred to as the "Giggle Loop". Luckily I was able to avoid to much damage for I was able to stop a minute later and run away. At least I was told later, that the widow said right off that her husband must have planned it that way, some big exit. It was just like him, he was a comedian after all.

Another funeral that I did, and I can say I am embarrassed I've played for but I will share it anyway. Why, well I can say that it was the funeral director's fault, but one for the books non the less, for I was called at the very last minute to play for a funeral near me. The original bagpiper called it off because he had received a better paying job offer. Not good for him! Anyway so I changed and drove down to the graveyard where I was supposed to play. I walked into the funeral office that was there and asked where I needed to go for this funeral. The gentleman that was there told me where it was and that I was right on time so I drove up the road and got ready. I was warming up for about 10 minutes when this gentleman came up and said that it was great to have me here though he didn't know someone had arranged for me to be there. I continued to warm up and when the minister got there spoke with him about what I was supposed to do. He didn't even know that I was going to play, but thought it was great. I played a wee bit at the beginning and after the service. The widow came up to me and thanked me for the great playing but was interested to know who hired me. I told her that I was rung up about two hours ago to come and play and didn't catch the name of the person who called me. "That's fine, no problem" is what she said to me and walked off to get into her car. I walked over to my car and drove to the front gate, when the funeral director walked out with a wee bit grin on his face. I was told with an embarrassing face that I played for the wrong funeral. The one I was supposed to play for was on the other side of the graveyard, and that the name was different then I was original told on the phone. I couldn't believe it. Unluckily that funeral had finished about 10 minutes before the one I did, so I didn't get a chance to talk to the person that really did ask me to come and play. The director laughed and told me not to worry about it, but I did. Man I was both mad and embarrassed about this, and made sure that I never did anything like that again and made sure I got everything almost in triplicate before I went anywhere. Of course, my wife may contradict that, the many times I have had to call her to verify I was in the right place and at the right time because no one is there yet. I get a wee bit panicky now because of that instance.

While living in Cumbria, I was once asked to play for a gentleman who had passed away recently. I got together with the widow and went over what they wanted done. It was easy stuff except they wanted me to play during the whole funeral, off near the edge of the graveyard. Luckily, this graveyard was out in the middle of nowhere so my playing wouldn't be a problem. However I did discovered a bit of a problem as soon as I got there. The graveyard was hilly and had a bit of a problem with gophers and moles—there were so many holes around the place that I had to keep an eye out when I walked. The signal came for me to start playing so I slowly walked the perimeter of the graveyard going through tune after tune that could be played at a funeral. The closest I would get to the funeral party when I was playing was about fifty feet away, since they were near the edge. But I kept on playing as I walked near them, keeping a close eye on the ground. As I neared the funeral party, I happened to look over to check on the progress of everything when I caught the look of someone in the party. They waved to me. I nodded back to them and I looked forward to watch where I was going. Well, I shouldn't have looked over to the funeral party because as I looked back to watch my footing, I fell right into a hole. Now, this hole wasn't a hole made by a mole or a gopher; no, it was a human-made hole, one for a casket that was going to be filled later the next morning. I fell in face first and, oh yes, it hurt. I could only guess what the funeral party heard coming from me. "Du da bo baaaaaaa" as I fell in. That person that had waved at me, of course saw me fall in and he ran over (laughing) to see if I was okay. Luckily, the hole had filled in with a bit of water, so that cushioned my fall according to the gentleman. He helped me up and I got right back into playing, after I cleaned the mud off my chanter and one of the drones that decided to collect some mud inside the opening. I must have looked a fright as the funeral concluded.

The last funeral that comes to mind to share with you was one that I did that wasn't funny, actually it is very personal to me. But it must be shared for we have all had something similar happen in our lives. It all started when I was leaving my house to play for another wedding on a Saturday and my mother-in-law came running out telling me to stop. She told me that my best friend was killed the night before. I couldn't believe it, but I had a job to do so I left to go do the wedding I was hired for, which was in the end a very long wedding for I was just not there. It was odd but not even a week earlier he and I had talked about playing the pipes for him if anything ever happened, so when I was asked by his wife to play the pipes for the funeral I couldn't say no, as he loved to hear me play. I had played for there wedding a couple of years before and he was my best friend so of course I was happy to do this, but I was worried that I might have a problem. I had never played for someone's funeral that I had known so well. On the day of the funeral I dressed up in my military uniform as he was an American Marine and I wanted to show respect to him and the military, and it was to be held at the Veteran's Cemetery. I always dressed in my military uniform when I did a funeral of other military members to show my respect. My wife and I showed up at the graveyard which was a military graveyard near Seattle. I warmed up and spoke to the honor guard that was there, asking them to make sure everything went well and share the importance of this event. Of course it did go fine, as I worked with these lads all the time. I knew they knew their business. I stood on the hill behind the gravesite and listened to the speeches, and then during the gun salute I started to play his favorite tunes. It was the hardest thing I believe I had ever done. I cried so hard that night. It was very hard to think he was gone as I had just talked to him the night prior to his death. A week later I was due to leave to teach in Asia. The day before I left to go to Asia, I went to the grave site and gave my friend the final salute, a dram of scotch. It was the least I could do for him!

It's also at funerals that I've found some of the worst priests, ministers and people performing. Some know what they are doing, some don't. The ones that do, let the families do what they want out of respect, the ones that don't, well you know. I can say that at some, families wanted to either kill the priest, or kiss him. Some I believe wanted to throw the priest into the hole, too, because of his, well, stupidity on the formalities of a funeral. Got to love being human!

EASY RIDERS

When I was young I believe I was about 15 years old or near that, I was asked by a friend of mine in school if I could help his older brother out for his wedding. I had no problem in this as I was about to move and wanted to see some of the people that were going to be at this wedding. I got together at the local pub with my friend and his brother, the lad's girlfriend came by later in the hour. We started by talking about what it would be like moving to another part of the world for a while for I was soon to move to the US for a bit of time. When we got to talking about the ceremony, I found out that my friend and groom to be were going to dress up in his local motor cycle gang jacket and have the ceremony at the local club house for the gang. I was pretty much up for anything and meeting a motorcycle gang on the good day was sounding pretty cool. They pretty much wanted a normal wedding, me walking in the bride, standing off the side then walking to the two out afterwards. Pretty easy, it was going to a fun wedding I thought. At the rehearsal it went off just like normal. No problems, as far as I could tell and no complaints from the bride or groom. The day of the wedding the weather became really hot, over 26 degrees celsius, I remember because a number of elderly people had died due to the heat that day in the local hospital. I drove up to the gang's clubhouse and warmed up. This day because of the heat it didn't take that long to warm up the pipes however, I also had to take off my jacket because of the heat. I started to notice that many of the guests were wearing leather and drove up on cycles at this point. I did think though; it was going to get hot in that hall especially with all that leather! I walked the bride in, the wedding went off very normal, and then the surprised came. While walking the couple out people started throwing condoms, luckily not used ones but none the less they were open, as well as chains at the couple, ouch!. I guess it was something this gang did for fun however I had to do quite a bit of ducking, to avoid getting hurt. I did have to remove a few of those condoms afterwards, stuck to my uniform. I remember hearing about this couple now having three kids and living in Wales somewhere still not sure if they are in the club but sounds like fun!

The next wedding that comes to mind was with a motorcycle gang in the United States years later. Maybe cycle gangs liked the heat because again this one was a hot one as well, or maybe it felt that way because of all the leather, once again. This was almost like the other except that I would just stand off at the back and play while the couple walked in and the then walked out. I played normal tunes for them, nothing special but again I was surprised, for when they walked down the isle this time they were not assaulted by sexual things like the condoms but with weapons. It's the American thing for people to walk around with weapons in their belts, but these wedding guests were packing enough to take on the local army base. So as the couple completed their vows and regular wedding stuff I was to start playing. As soon as I filled my bag up, as I do to start playing, I noticed that people were pulling out their weapons. Not big machine guns or anything like that, but just small pistols. As soon as I started playing, people starting shooting up into the ceiling, scaring the hell out of me, not because of the shooting, nor the fact that the room wasn't that big, but the fact that if one bullet bounced off something up above, someone was dead. Now I must admit this did cause me to pause and reflect as to weather to continue on however I did start my pipes up again and I slowly edge my way out of the path of the bride and groom, they soon passed me so I went to leave. Yes, the couple had forgotten to tell me about this and gave me an extra tip for not running away which I had strongly considered at the time. I thanked them and got in the car and drove as fast as I could, because people were walking out of the church at this point looking a wee bit messed up. What a day I thought and time to get the hell out of here while I could. Just a tip if there is going to be anything unusual like guns being fired off you might want to let any vendors that are hired for the wedding a heads up on what to expect!

CASTLE WEDDINGS

Castle weddings can be mystic and distinctive giving a diversity and uniqueness to any wedding. Playing in castles whether in Scotland or England, as I did when I was younger, even one created in the United States a few years ago is something very special for a bagpiper for it ties in with history. Being a historian has made it even more of a delight to play at a historical monument such as the many castles in England and Scotland. While serving in the British Army I was given permission to branch out and play for private functions. Of course, playing at the Edinburgh Castle was always the climax of any bagpiper's career. On three occasions I had the opportunity to play in the great hall of the castle. If you haven't seen it, take a look at it on their web site, www.historic-scotland.gov.uk. The hall, though not the biggest does give the person an idea what medieval halls looked like in Scotland 600 years ago.

The wedding I remember the most was playing for a small time actor from Canada that had come over to Scotland and marry his long love girlfriend of around 10 years. I was asked to play for them, as well as arrange all the music that they wanted, which included not only me but flutes, violins and guitars, making the ceremony a musical enchantment. It took me about two weeks to get everything together, but luckily Edinburgh is a musical city, and has loads of musicians at ones beck and call. After gathering the musicians together I was able to convince the groom to have a small rehearsal because just going for it, well who knows what could happen. I was to start playing over by St. Briget's chapel over by the wall and slowly walk over toward the Great Hall where the Bride would then pop out of a side door, in today's times it's a door that goes into the café. Back then the café was not opened yet. Then walk slowly into the hall, playing the song, the "75th Farwell to Gibraltar", being the groom's favorite. This is not usually a tune played at weddings, but hey what can I do. As I got inside I was to walk her up to the great fireplace where the groom was to be waiting. After the wedding I was to play for them as they walked into the courtyard for about 10 minutes. Before and after I played, the rest of the musicians were playing either Bach or Mozart and the occasional Proclaimer's tune. This is where every person working a wedding must be prepared for something to happen. In Scotland as in any place in the world, the weather has a tendency to change usually every five minutes and not always for the best. The rehearsal two days prior was a beautiful Scottish day, chilly but the sun was out, but then as the weather does in Scotland it changed for the worst. The weather continued on this course until the day of the ceremony.

The bride, however was willing to keep plans as they were, so I played for my 10 minutes over by the wall, getting soaked from the rain water coming up over the wall and down on me. As I walked toward the bride, another thing for a piper to keep in mind when it might be windy is too wear something underneath your kilt if you don't want to be embarrassed, my kilt flew up in front of the bride causing her to laugh ludicrously. Not because of what she saw, or at least I hoped not, but because it was just a funny thing to see happen. Of course I couldn't do anything about it, but continued to play. After the wedding, both the groom and bride came to me and thanked me for all the help and for adding laughter to the bride's day, for it put her at ease. Today, even though it goes against tradition sometimes depending on the ceremony I still wear something underneath my kilt, just to avoid that uneasiness again.

The next castle wedding was one too remember as well as it was held near Edinburgh at a castle called Craigmiller. This old castle was famous for being in so many battles during the medieval ages and for having historical figure like Mary Queen of Scots, stayed there. The young couple, or really it was a young man and his older bride to be, I believe she was at least 20 years older than he was wanted a peaceful ceremony with a touch of sophistication. The ceremony was to take place in the main courtyard of the castle which was covered in grass and was to be cut the very day of the ceremony. With a lot of castle locations it's impossible to have a rehearsal at the site due to schedule conflicts and costs. Being a person that is allergic to cut grass, I made sure that I took the right medicine before hand, so that I did not sneeze through the ceremony. So keep that in mind with grass, food or whatever you might think might be a problem for you whether you are the piper, musician, or in the wedding party, even the bride and groom must remember to consider this in their planning. After getting together with this couple three weeks prior to the wedding and having a wedding rehearsal the day before, not at the castle where we could test the ground, as they were holding some type of ceremony themselves. We had it at a pub in the village of Duddingston. The day of the ceremony I was to walk the parents in, then the candle lighters, as well as the bride's maids, then the groom and his men, as well as any family. I was going to do a lot of walking that day, so I made sure I wore the correct shoes. The bride was going to come in from behind everyone else; she was waiting in a large car out in the car park. It was a wonderful day for a wedding, birds were chirping, the sun was out, in Edinburgh this is great even with cut grass, everything seemed to be going just right. However, here is where it went all wrong though, I was walking in front of the bride playing, looking at the people in the crowd to see their expressions, when I saw many drop their things and run past me. I kept playing as I turned around, only to see that the bride had stepped into a hole, not a deep one, just enough to make a person fall. Her dress went up and over her, so everything was seen. I kept on playing, thinking at the time that it was just a trip and she would be on her feet shortly. However that was not the case, we found out later that she had broken her ankle. At this point, I stopped and waited to find out what to do. I felt bad about her however as her husband to be ran over laughing, I had to giggle a bit because and even the bride though in pain was laughing. She wanted to keep going, so the whole crowd, including the priest moved the altar back about 20 feet back to there were the bride was. We sat the bride in a chair and continued on with a really fast ceremony. Truthfully it was only about a two minute ceremony, though it was planned to be at least a 20 minutes. After the wedding, I just walked over to the wall and played while she and her new husband went to the hospital, entertaining the guests. I received a call three days later from the groom. He thanked me for the music, and I was posted an extra payment for my patience. In reality, I wasn't really patient. I was just surprised it went forward however I reassured them that it was nothing unusual. Sometimes you just have to say a wee bit white lie, not for the money, but to make the couple feel better.

Of all the castles weddings that I've done, looking back, this one was probably the funniest of them all. If you've been to Tantallon Castle in Scotland you know how big that castle is. This ceremony was going to be in the outer courtyard where the dovecot was. A dovecot is where the lords or knights kept birds for their meals. It was a beautiful dovecot with a massive field around it. The problem started when Historic Scotland told the bride's mother who was arranging the wedding, that there was going to be construction in the car park or something in that area. However in order to ensure that her daughter was happy she went ahead with the plans for this is what she really wanted, if I recall correctly. Remember though, at this time weddings in the United Kingdom were only legal if they were held in a churches or at the maturates office, so most weddings I did outside of churches were just for show and a civil ceremony was held either later or earlier. When we arrived for the rehearsal we found that the car park was fine, we thought, well they much have fixed it pretty fast, unusual for Scotland. We kept walking nearer to the castle only to find that the front gate of the outer wall was boarded up, so when the guard told us that that the castle was getting fixed it was a vast understatement. We didn't know what to do but I asked the guard if we could at least go in and practice. He said we shouldn't but let us in, which was so nice. I wish I remembered his name because he helped me in the next instance as well. Originally I was to start in the main entry way and walk to the location of the dovecot out on the field, however the bride was pretty upset with the construction for it interfered with the perfect picture. The mother of the bride was willing to do almost anything to ensure this wedding went off as her daughter wanted, I think, for she was on the phone instantly and I assume everything was arranged for we then move to the interior court yard. So instead of walking from the gate out I was going to start playing from outside the main wall with the bride behind me, then walk in. The groom and the guests which were only 20 or so would be standing in the middle of the yard. This bride was a joy to work with; because she was bubbly and had a great idea of what she wanted in life. Now here however is where the problems started to arise, for when we moved to the wedding itself, the bride decided to get really drunk before the ceremony. However I was totally unaware that this was the case, as I'm terrible at seeing things like that. This time I was thinking about keeping an eye on the bride, as much a possible especially considering what had happened before. So here I am playing, and I turn to make sure she's walking, oh she was walking, but in the wrong direction. The man that was escorting her in, motioned for me to keep playing, so I did, repeating the current tune over and over because it took abut 10 minutes to get her to walk in the right direction.

So here I am playing slowly and I mean slowly so that we can walk in. Now you must understand that as you come into the castle there is a slight rise, which wasn't that hard to walk up, but man was she drunk so she didn't make it up this rise. She walked up the hill only to roll back down. Some of her guests ran over, the escort said to keep playing. I walked over to an area and did just that, however now playing tunes that just hit me, some slow, fast, and even some jigs, while I watched the whole thing take place. As I played, I saw the bride getting picked up like she was a wounded soldier and brought out to the car park. Some of the guests stood around, some were even laughing at this whole thing. This is where the Historic Scotland guy helped the people put her in the car. I just kept on playing, which was great because as some pipers and musicians know, once you get into the rhythm, you can just keep going and going. I must have played at least five minutes after the whole crowd had left. I walked out to my car, and thanked the guard. He gave me a note asking me to go to the church where the main ceremony was taking place in two hours. I wasn't originally supposed to play there, nevertheless what the hell nothing was going on and it would be interesting to see what happened next. This is where I thought the whole thing was just getting interesting. I came up to the church, where the mother came to me thanking me for the help. She then told me that her daughter was drunk, she could speak, but walking was out. So they had acquired a wheel chair to roll her in to the church. That's not funny, but what happened during the ceremony at the church was just great. I played while they rolled her in, however at this time she looked a bit out of it and during the ceremony she just woke up and started to roll away saying it was wrong, wrong, wrong. She didn't realize that she was up two steps on the altar area, but she did when she fell over wheelchair and all. Anyway, she never really got to say "I do", because now she was in the hospital for she had broken her wrist and sprained her shoulder. The next time I saw her which was a few days later, she had a bandage over her nose, her wrist and right arm was bandaged up with a sling. Man I felt bad. As for her husband to be who was with her was laughing. He went on to tell me when we met that she was a major accident prone girl always constantly hurting herself and he didn't except the rest of his life with her to be any different. I could see why!

Knight in Shinning Something

Medieval weddings or ones like them can be both fun and funny, for many reasons. One, being an historian, they are funny because of the inaccuracy of the clothing or costumes. Many people believe they know exactly what the medieval world was like from wedding to daily events, some even claiming to be able to tell you exactly what it was to be there. Something that I can say I've discovered even with professors at certain universities in Scotland, with them saying like the battle at Bannockburn wasn't the turning point for Scottish history, which every other historian knows to be true. No one can say that they know everything about the medieval world. Anyway these type of weddings are both amusing and out of the ordinary to watch, so I had to write something down about the ones that I did.

These stories are made up of weddings, parties and events that I either did either wearing medieval clothing myself, or was asked to play at some medieval performance. Not to say that the groups I played for were strange or odd, no, they were just into that way of life in such an extend that they actually lived it to a degree, making it hard to tell them when they are doing something that potentially is inaccurate. However, the point of a wedding is that everyone has a good time and that the bride and groom get to live out their fantasy. I found these weddings so enjoyable because it was great fun watching the different ways people add in their individual touches to their weddings. Going from Russian, to Scottish of course, to even an Arab style wedding, I was in the thick of things.

The first wedding that comes to mind in the medieval theme was taking place in England in the early 1480's, oh sorry early 1980's. It was near the Hereford area of England, which is one of my favorite places, really. Not much there in the way of anything bad you know, mountains in Wales are near, the forests are great, and Hereford is a city that is just the right size for me. Plus my uncle lives near there. I was asked to play the pipes in the morning for a wedding, while the fog was still sitting on the ground. Pretty nice I thought. I thought when confronted with a great idea by the couple or person hiring me to see if they can get someone to take pictures of me. I forgot many, many times to do just this and to this day don't have pictures that captured such memories of many weddings, parties and more that I have done over the years. Since meeting my wife I have been able to increase these captured moments however the early years are what is lost.

In any case playing on the moor or field is what they were trying to achieve, which I was told later was just beautiful to hear. Though I've heard, from many professionals that even though bagpipes are loud, they still have the same problem with the airwaves like every other wind instrument. If the wind is not moving in the direction of the people you want to hear it they are not going to. I heard myself very well that day, but I'm surprised anyone else did as the fog was in the way which usually tends to settle the sound of the pipes to where they are not allowing them to drift on the wind, making very eerie.

Then later that day, for this was an all day event for me. I've heard from many bagpipers and many other musicians that they are taken advantage of many times. Playing longer than the originally requested, as the contract states, or at the last moment some position is changed without your knowledge causing for an adjustment that involves more time and energy. Don't get me wrong those kinds of events are usually the most incredible, however a piper does not plan to bring food or extra water in these such events. If you do get hired for such an event, make sure the client realizes that your time is precious and you need to be taken care of, for after hours on your feet it has a tendency to wear you down. Without experience, many performers will just do what they are asked without realizing the expenditure or dilemma it will cause in the long run.

Anyway back to the wedding. Since the day was set aside for the pre-wedding party celebration, the night was when the wedding itself was to take place. I was to walk the bride in, who was on a horse, of course, and then play when the groom came in. I learned from early on, that no wedding is the same, except I think if you're in Las Vegas even then there are still variances. The wedding was exceptional. They had people dressed up like cavaliers from the English Civil War, to people dress up like Robin Hood. I was dressed up over my jumper (sweater) in a Scottish medieval dress such as the one you would see in the movie, 'Rob Roy'. Now the really memorable part of this whole wedding was the weather for in this part of England especially this part, it rains a lot. So when the fog lifted, it rained the rest of that day. Now bagpipes coming from Scotland are used to the rain, so I wasn't worried much about them getting ruined. On the other hand I wasn't ok. I had on only a jumper, but by then that was soaked and did not provide any kind of warmth. So here I was, wet and not doing that well, but the client was happy, even though they were wet as well. That's the most important part of any wedding, that the bride and groom are happy for it is so hard to satisfy every single family member, remembering however that it is your day makes all the difference.

This next wedding was probably the most memorable medieval wedding that I have done since everyone was dressed up in Elizabethan dresses and uniforms. The precise look in the uniforms was just incredible to see and touch. This couple had spent thousands of pounds sterling getting it done right. The bride wanted herself to look like Queen Elizabeth, which she did in the end. The groom, who wanted to look like, in some funny way Henry the 8th, for he was not at all fat or short, but wanted to look the part and was nicely dressed himself. The couple has in the end purchased me a costume. At first I thought this was a wee bit odd for me to wear, a jesters costume, not the Scottish one that I usually wear. Their thoughts were that Scotsman didn't look like what I was wearing at the time period they were portraying. They wanted to keep it very authentic. For some reason they must have thought that I had some comical part in the wedding. I played some great music, some Beethoven, Bach, yes they can be played on the bagpipes, and even some tunes from the Scottish military music list. These people had also asked their guests to dress up in the era they wanted, and most did. The food was great, as well as everyone else's part. I noted that day there were a number of other musicians and wanted to make sure I didn't try to interfere with anyone else's music. The only thing that came about at this particular wedding was my getting attacked by drunken guests in the reception. They all thought I was a girl or something for they kept hitting on me or wanting to play a funny tune. They must have been so pissed that it was making their eyes go. I tried to be nice however giving any excuse I could come up with, I had to do something to do or somewhere to be, anywhere really.

The next wedding that comes to mind is one of the scariest weddings when it comes to medieval weddings. It was the one I did while I was living in New England during the middle 80's for a while. Here I was asked to work for a group of medieval people who wanted to do a Celtic type wedding. At first being the historian I was very interested in this. I have read and studied the Celtic ways of performing a wedding by this time, or what historians have thought they might have been performed like. This wedding though was everything but right. Right off the bat I was not having a good time because they didn't pay me any deposit and being young I wasn't sure what to do. Just a note, when asking for a deposit make sure it's in your contract that you take a certain amount paid by a certain time to avoid conflict, especially when multiple bookings become involved. At this wedding, I ended up begging in way to get my money which is really unbecoming and make one look so unprofessional. I just wasn't sure how to handle it at the time. This of course is very embarrassing for me and them.

Back to the wedding, I had the opportunity to talk with the groom briefly and set up the particulars. However, when I requested the opportunity to sit down with the couple together, for it is usually my custom to talk first hand with both parties to see what they are both looking for, so that no one becomes disappointed, the groom however said it was the Celtic way not to converse with the bride. I couldn't even talk to her or call her, which I knew even then was not right. So here I was getting contracted for a wedding that I would never talk to the centre point of the ceremony itself. This has happened on occasion but only when my playing was a surprise. Most wedding couples I meet always think of a wedding as a joint effort or that it's for the family, however in the end, I believe it is mainly for the bride, for it is her day. She's going to live with someone for the rest of her life, she deserves something special.

The day of the rehearsal came, and I was able to finely hear what was wanted, as the groom really haven't told me much up until that point, being that I had talked him only briefly. This is why today I always have a contract with all the particulars ahead of time. So I drove up to the wedding site, which was on top of this big hill outside of the town of Norwich, Connecticut. The weather seemed fine, but not the couple. They were fighting about what they wanted, the rest of the crew (the wedding party) as they called themselves just sat off to the side and were drinking. Subsequently I walked over to the crew, started talking and they gave me a drink. Therefore I ended up getting a wee bit light headed if you know what I mean by the time the fight ended. I couldn't believe they were going through with it, fighting in front of people they both cared about and hired to do work at their wedding. The groom was going to dress up as a Celtic warrior but with a wee bit flare as I guess you can call it. It consisted of him wearing a kilt, or rather a kind of great kilt, more a large piece of plaid fabric with a brooch at one shoulder, however the interesting part was the shoes were a normal every day style of boot. Then they finally got everything settled I hardly had a spot in the wedding, playing them out of the area at the end of the ceremony. They believed it would only be 1-2 minutes of playing. The next day was the wedding, wouldn't you believe it, they ended up fighting again, so almost all of the "crew" was drunk again just sitting there waiting for them to wrap things up and of course this included me, for it tends to make things a wee bit unnerving to watch a couple fight. The groom even pulled out his sword and was swinging it around almost hitting his wife to be. The wedding finally happened and I played my part, however of course making some minor mistakes because of my head being a wee bit light headed. I have gotten drunk at only a few weddings, not the best thing to do at a wedding, but these are usually good close friends and only after I have played my part. So only the weddings that I know it is ok to do so. There are many weddings that I been too in the medieval world, I guess you can call it, that I have felt out of place.

After I had done about five medieval weddings I went out and worked with some seamstress that could make me three types of costumes that were medieval in nature. The first one which was the most important to me was the Scottish Highlander costume. This one, if you look in the history books was the one you are likely to see what a Highlander would wear say during the 1745 Rebellion or a wee bit bit earlier. I even had some small flintlocks pistols to go with the uniform. I also had a basket hilt sword that I had received from my family's home in Cumbria or the north-western part of England. It was left, or taken from the Scots that were in the area so many years ago. I loved this costume for the number one reason that it looked the best as well as being the most comfortable to wear. The next was what I called the total Scottish barbarian look, someone that looks like they are from Scotland around 1000 or even earlier. Here I had a huge sword, and many knives to go with it.

One wedding which I'll talk about in a bit, I even wore makeup, this wedding took place right after Mel Gibson's "Braveheart". Another wedding was more of a Renaissance look than looking like a Scotsman. I didn't have the tight leggings, (thank god), but I did have the big puffy shirt and jacket. That one was hard to play in because it interfered with my bag when I tried to start playing. The jacket would just push the bag down so that I couldn't get it under my arm well enough and I looked like I had a hump coming out of my side or back. Hated those pictures when I did see them. The one thing that I say that a piper must be careful with when it comes to many of these medieval groups that are around the world. They all believe that they are retelling the true story through the look when it comes to what ever look they are trying to achieve. I have seen Scotsman wearing clothes that were Japanese looking or German knights wearing something that looked Arab in nature. All this is fine for it is their wedding however remember to be careful what you say, they take offense to what you say especially when telling that is not appropriate for the time period. I told one guy once that he was wearing the wrong type of knife. It was a Japanese type knife and if his character had gone to Japan during the 1400's which I found very hard to believe, later yes but being that most Scotsman didn't venture that far from Scotland at that time period, and to visit the Far East at the time he said he was representing, well you get my meaning.

Medieval weddings are a great way to have fun with your mind, stepping into a fantasy world of sorts. One wedding you do will give you ideas for another wedding or event you do later. These next stories happened when I was asked to come play at some special events. The first one was while I was living in New England for while. This particular medieval group had a huge event each year that takes place in western Pennsylvania near Pittsburgh. Being that the event takes place at the hottest time of the year a lot of people would just wear light clothes and even going as far in some areas to wear no clothes at all, must be claiming their Pictish heritage. Anyway, they have this huge field battle where if every knight and man-at-arms in the camp went out on the field, it could have up to 500 men and women fighting. I was asked to pipe leading this band of Scottish, Irish, and Welsh fighters out to the field from their camp that was about half a mile away. It was a lot of fun playing for the man in front walking with me. He was a gizzer playing a duke, which caused much attention by the on lookers and it was fascinating to see this huge column of men walking towards the battle field. I walked them out into the middle of the field with all the pomp and fireworks that go with a medieval knight and battle. When I was finished I walked off the field and watched like a spectator eating a picnic lunch. I had fun and after an hour the side I played for began to win the battle and many knights from the other side who were killed were walking past me. Well let's just say that human anger sometimes even takes the best of people because one knight was so mad when he walked past me he pushed me over, almost breaking my pipes. I told the duke after the battle and he and his knights searched for the guy, but nothing happened except that I was given a field commission of baron. So nice for me! Oh yes, the wedding happened, but in the middle of the battle. It only took two minutes before the bride and groom got their rings, vows and ran out, before the rest of the knights and men got nervous and charged.

Years later in Europe I was asked to walk this clan out to the field of battle, but it had an obstacle in the way, a river that was about 3 feet deep. Not a fast river, but enough to cause some problems for some of the knights. When I reached the river playing the battle tune of the Donald's, one tune I loved playing, I kept on playing even as I entered the river. Every once and while my chanter would go under water making the most interesting sounds, a few people were able to capture it on film, I think. Hopefully that didn't catch my kilts rising up with the water as I went walking in. Glad there were any flesh biting fish in there I might have lost something, so Hollywood like in the end!

Another wedding that comes to mind with a medieval theme was to be held in the desert area of Washington State. It was hot like all deserts are but this time it was also humid, which I thought was a wee bit weird. It had rained in the region for three days straight so the wetness must have stayed. The wedding itself was to take place on top of a knoll where the minister, myself and the guests were to stand or sit if possible and wait for the main wedding party to arrive. The nearest car park was about a quarter of a mile away and it was a trek to get to this location, but the couple had met there while hiking with friend's years earlier and had always loved it. I couldn't blame them, the view was incredible. So when we saw the dust track of cars coming in, we hoped it was them. A gentleman had been asked to sit off to the side and provide water in case anyone needed it, the only problem was that more people showed up then there was bottles of water. What started out being a nice day in the beginning ended up being a scorcher and many people were needing water fast. Now a days I always get water before I go to a wedding, you never know when you need it but like I have said before you can sometimes be unprepared even with planning. The couple arrived about 10-15 minutes late because of farm animals on the road. As soon as I saw them I started to play the tune, 'Loch Lomond' which the bride really loved. I played it for about five minutes then moved on to 'Mairi's Wedding' which was name of the mother of bride. When they walked down the aisle it was interesting to see the couple walking the wrong way down the aisle, towards me instead of the altar. They decided to take the time to meet with guests before hand even stopping me and offering some water, which was very cold and so needed. So nice of them and why this one sticks in my memory as a wedding that went fine with no one passing out from the heat. I believe however I lost about 10 pounds of water weight that day I know the bride and groom did, they both wore 18th century clothing and looked like they were going to die after the wedding. This is really the only think that made this a medieval wedding.

Recently my wife and I thought it would be fun to join a group in Scotland the represented what life was like in the middle ages. The group performed for Historic Scotland which is a public funded group that takes cares of historic building all over Scotland. This group did demos around the country which included all sorts of the fun things for children giving them a stronger understanding of history. I was asked to come to the castle of Caerlaverock to walk the Scots into battle as this would have been done during the 14th century as in the real battle, just with less people now and lots of less blood. The performance went well and I was a big hit. Afterwards because some of my family was in attendance, I was asked to walk into the castle and play for them and some of the other audience members that stayed after the battle. So here I was standing on a balcony playing, and the music was bouncing everywhere, for this castle was an unusual one, shaped in the form of a triangle. So many pictures were being taking of me not just by my family but Americans, Germans and English that had come over for holiday. It was a great feeling and its great for families to get outdoors and see living history.

My last medieval wedding took place just as I was writing this book. I didn't think getting into the wedding would make it into this, but it did. This group were a funny sort of people and when I mean funny you'll understand soon. Most of the people in the wedding group I believe were normal to a degree, as they dressed mostly in Japanese samurai uniforms. Most of them looked like they had time warped from 15th century Japan. Some even were speaking Japanese which I can understand a bit of, as I had learned some from friends who were Japanese and I had visited Japan many times. During the reception they had dancers, taiko drumming, which I love to watch, and even a few actors sword fighting. Most of the wedding was to be a Zen Buddhist ceremony and in Japanese, so I was wondering why I was going to be there. Turns out that the bride was half Scottish and that her mum was from Glasgow. My part was very easy, walk the bride in. Sounds simple and easy right? It was but I didn't really think that many in her family wanted me there. I can understand why. I was a surprise to the audience and only the bride and groom knew I was going to be there. She thought it would be nice for her mum's ancestry to also represented there. I wore a simple uniform just nothing to outshine the rest of wedding party. Have done that in the past by mistake, you learn pretty fast not to do that.

So even before the wedding started, I'm standing off to the side in the back with the bride when her uncle came over and pretty much started to insult me. The bride took it in stride and pushed him away, telling me he was drunk. No worries, I told her and got back into focus when another member of the family came up behind me and lifted my kilt saying something pretty bad in Japanese which I heard but didn't know it was towards me. Now at first I didn't know my kilt was up, but when the bride gasped and said something sharp and hard at this person I turned around and pushed my kilt down and walked over to another area to wait. Let's just say that after the wedding I got a big tip, from her mostly to apologize for what her family and friends had done to me, because they were all drunk and didn't like a guy in a dress being at her wedding. It was no worries, I just had a great time being there seeing all the beauty of the Japanese culture and to see it in person. I did get out of there pretty fast when I saw a few of her family walking toward me with mad looks.

Though this next one isn't a wedding or a medieval event, it has to do with history. For a few years I was asked to play the bagpipes while walking in British soldiers doing a recreation of the Battle of Lexington, Concord, and Bunker Hill in Boston, Massachusetts. There were only a few people who did the reenactment but it was fun to do it. Of course, bagpipes weren't played during this period of early American history but the noise is what the actors wanted in order to get the news out there and to draw more attention to the event.

A few years later, when I was living north of Seattle, I decided to do almost the same thing, but on a smaller stage. This time, a group of us dressed as Brits and as rebels to reenact the Battle of Concord and Lexington, choosing to reenact the British retreat from Lexington to end in a huge music celebration for the 4th of July. I was always pretty good at sewing things but I decided that even I wasn't that good in coming up with an authentic Scottish uniform for that time period, so I hired a dress maker to make me a piper's uniform. A few dollars later I had a nice red coat and white vest to go with it. We practiced and practiced to make sure the battles went well, however, as we know, nothing goes well when fake muskets are used. I had a black powder pistol I had received from my family years earlier so I carried that while I was playing, in the hopes that I could fire it off just once. I also got a friend who played the drums to come along as we marched the Brits down the road. What a sight it must have been—bright red coats and bright white pants marching down the high street of the town. We even played for the 4th of July parade that happened later that day. It was during the last battle, which was supposed to be Lexington, where I came up with the idea to go a wee bit crazy. When I say crazy I didn't pull out my sword and start killing people, no, I would drop my pipes on the ground and charge the rebels in front of me. Well, you can guess what happened. I died, yes! And it was fun to do. The audience went crazy for it, seeing a British soldier charging forward screaming like a mad man and being taken down. Just imagine what a Scot would act like in battle. Of course, the line of rebels would all fire at me when I did, so the noise was huge. I'm such an actor for the audience.

MERLIN AND THE STONES

When it comes to weddings that bring back the old Celtic ways, as some like to say, by using rocks or rather stone circles that where put up to represent the compass they always end up being a wee bit amusing in my opinion. One stone circle wedding was consisting of four main stones that faced the four directions of the map with smaller stones in between these all in the form of a circle. The wedding consisted of the wedding party dressed in somewhat modern but with a medieval touch to the clothes. I found that the groom's tux was a wee bit funny, to see him wearing his kilt but with a beer gut sticking out, something that really is embarrassing to many people wearing a kilt. I was going to pipe in the groom and the groom's party but had to wait as the minister blessed each of the four major stone by sprinkling water and sweeping aside a section of the circle for us to walk through. No there was no actual boundary there just an imaginary line. Once we walked through the circle this was to be closed again. The same thing was done when the bride came through however this time I just stood off to the side and played. Once the bride was at the altar or head stone a musician played different instrument to each of the main stones, one a recorder was played to one, a didgeridoo was played to another, a penny whistle to another and final a harp at the last, head stone. Finally, before the actually vows could be exchanged a belly dancer blessed each stone by dancing around each and every stone while a musician played recorder. This belly dancer, not the best looking I thought, but did certain things that made the men in the audience move around a bit by bending this way or that into unusual forms. After the blessing was completed the vows were exchanged but now wait this is not the end of this unusual wedding because after the couple's exchange of vows and the bride gave a flute tribute to the groom followed by the binding of hands. She did a wonderful job playing the flute, and the hand binding went ok but most ministers are not very familiar with the hand binding tradition so they tend to fumble a bit. Some I've heard from couples even have refused to do it, as they believe it it's a pagan tradition or something evil. I find it interesting that many people that I've met believe they all know the right way to do hand binding ceremony's, who really knows,really, because it was never written down by the ancient Celts, so we are all just guessing.

Now the walk out of the circle had to consist of much the same as the entry with a broom to sweep aside the circle so that the couple could exit properly. I then walked the bride and groom out of the circle at this point. Somewhere in this wedding I remember someone reading a story about something, not the traditional one you hear in a church ceremony, as it was unusual somehow, I don't remember except seeing a guest asleep while it was being read. This was a very long ceremony with much involved so one tends to drift a bit. My wife said later that she did the same as she was also at the wedding, just make sure you don't go too far, like falling a sleep. I didn't go that far but I remember thinking, oh please just hurry up. This was a cute couple and I played my best for them, but sometimes I wish I am more critical about who I work for. I was not fully aware of what would occur at this ceremony as there was no rehearsal and it showed. There were long pauses when no one knew what they were doing or where to go, again showing how important a rehearsal is for everyone. Rehearsals gives each person a clear understanding of what they need to do, where to be when and what will be involved in the ceremony. This also desolves surprises as there were in this one, it was a mess in the end. Even if it's for a small event a fast rehearsal can mean the whole of difference, they need to be done people. I've been to many weddings or events where they should have had a rehearsal, but did not. I just think that things run so much smoother when a rehearsal is held but it is sometimes funny how they do turn out no matter what.

The best stone circle wedding I did was near Edinburgh, just south of the city. A stone circle which later was made into a Roman fort, but they say it was a Neolithic house first. Castlelaw is a great wee bit hole in the ground, but because it's on top of a hill it can get incredibly cold up there. The bride's mother had rung up a friend of mine around noon a couple of days before the wedding, asking her about some logistical things in regards to the wedding, for she was coordinating the event. Somehow it slipped in asking her if she knew a good bagpiper. Well of course she gave my name, what a good friend! I got the call about 9pm that night and the mother just went off on what her daughter wanted. She didn't sound too happy about it really, however when I met her in addition to getting to know her I asked her what the problem was. She wasn't happy it wasn't the Christian thing to do getting married outside the church. I understood that but told her it's her daughter and we have to do what they want if we want to keep them as family. Well, that made her happier, I like to think anyway however she still ended up having a fight with her daughter at the dinner rehearsal and even walking out. She was in the wedding but her face was one that made people shift around, were all wondering what was going to happen. I remember years later watching an episode of "Home Improvement" where a friend of Tim's, the main character's wife came in and gave him that same look, I think they even called it "The Look". This face made all the men in the room freeze and hide. It matched her look exactly.

I was to walk the bride up the hill from the car park up toward the main area of the fort. Three things happened that day that even as I write make me laugh really hard today. First never trust the weather guy, he said that it would be a nice normal Scottish day in Edinburgh, no rain and wee bit wind. Well, it was raining like tomorrow would never come but the bride wanted to go ahead. Up until this time I hadn't met the groom yet, he was always working and couldn't meet me. Second thing that happened, the army which has a target practice range next to this historical fort and stone circle where also practicing. Now most of the time you just heard nothing but then a pop or snap, but this day probably because of the rain it sounded like a war going on over the next hill, machine guns, grenades, blowing up the works, an all out war. The kids in the audience where loving it but some weren't. Lastly the bride was walking up the hill, which was a pretty steep hill, and was hit in the face by a young boy's mud ball. He was playing off to the side and thought it would be funny. Oh man, did she try to kill him and to this day I've never seen him again, so I hope he left the country. As a result the groom is standing there and when she walked around the corner, oh what a face he made. Here is his bride to be covered in mud and looking terrible now. At first he thought she fell, but as she yelled at him over the rain, telling everyone else what happened. He just laughed as did many in the audience. Now playing in the rain is hard for pipers, mainly because the instrument gets wet, even an instrument from Scotland, of course, but it does make it hard to hold. Maybe it was a kid thing, I've never minded it, I love the rain, always have and I think I always will. This might be why it seemed I was always ordered to be the piper in the battalion when it was raining hard. However, considering the rain and the fact that I was trying not to laugh it was a very difficult day. After about 15 or so minutes into the wedding, the audience started to move toward the car park, even though the ceremony wasn't over, the rain just got heavier and heavier. The bride sees this and told the priest that he needed to hurry up. She didn't want her story to be that the bride was the last one to leave the wedding ceremony. He skipped about three parts of the ceremony and ended it right then. I struck up the pipes and walked them, carefully to the car park where they had a large car waiting for them. Let's just say that the wedding dinner was fun and simple, while the bride went home to take a shower and change. I think many people just wanted to get dry and warm anyway. I was asked to come to the hotel and do the same, but I didn't have anything to wear so I ended up wearing something one of the relatives had got from Princess Street during a tourist shopping trip. I showed up looking like a tourist so much fun and laughs I though. I always remember then that if the weather isn't looking that great, bring an extra set of clothing. Even if I didn't get invited somewhere after the wedding it was a must.

The next wedding that I did was near a stone circle or stone enclosure was a few years ago near Carlisle. This one of my favorite places to play the pipes as you can hear the music for miles and you are surrounded by hills of heather and sheep. I took my wife there on our honeymoon and we got a ton pictures. She is a huge fan of stone circles and Neolithic history so she loved it.

This wedding was very small in numbers just myself the bride and groom and two witnesses. I think this wedding was the best for a few reasons. The groom worked for the county government in Carlisle in the computer section of the city council. Therefore he knew computer things and he looked it too. Huge glasses, pocket protector and always had a bag with papers in it over his shoulder. Even at the wedding he brought this bag with him. I heard the bride comment later, at least he didn't wear it during the ceremony. The pocket protector was there though but now it was white and had a bow on it. Humor to the last! He and I talked a lot and became good friends. It's just too bad I lost in touch with him because I heard he had a load of children and they own their own company in Carlisle now. He told me that they wanted a small wedding so small that he was even thinking of having cut outs of themselves there and having me play for them. That would have been interesting in case someone came walking in and saw me playing for no one. I didn't have to play much for this one, they were a quiet bunch and the witnesses were friends. No family, well they told me right off when they hired me, because they hated their families and knew they wouldn't approve of what they were doing. Not the wedding but where it was. Therefore this was to make their families even madder. Love it! I stood off to the side and waited for my bit of the ceremony. The problem with so many places in this world is it's hard to keep the public out unless it's raining or something to do with the weather. While we are doing the ceremony and I see a coach of people drive up down the hill. I'm the only one so far that can see this and I knew we had at least 15 minutes to go in the ceremony but less for the coach to arrive. I raised my finger to the minister indicating I'd be back and darted off to intercept the people coming out of the coach. Then it hit me, they were Asian. I didn't know from where didn't care except they just had tons of cameras. I ran up and asked for the tour guide, he came over and I asked if they could wait for a few minutes until the wedding ceremony was over. He said no problem it would give him time to talk about the history of the area. He then turned around and I walked back up the hill. When I heard him explain to the tour group what was going on but instead of waiting they all ran forward and started taking pictures of the ceremony. The couple weren't mad at me or the situation, its just that the tour group was walking up and taking pictures right in their face. So as it turned out to be an even more interesting wedding after all.

The thing about weddings in Neolithic or ancient places like stone circle or forts is the tour groups often stop by unexpected. Unless the couple made the arrangements and even then it becomes difficult nothing could be done. Just need someone standing there in a police uniform saying 'Nothing to see here move along'.

WHAT SWEET MUSIC THEY MAKE

I guess one of the weirdest weddings for me so far is the one that I had to play for a group of vampires. This wedding was after I first moved to Seattle back in the 1990's. I was working at a video entertainment company part time just to make some extra money when I was asked by a co-worker to play the pipes for a friend. It was fun talking to the bride on the phone and she asked if I could meet up with her and her friends sometime later. I later thought what a great way to meet people especially when you are trying to meet someone to date. I wasn't seeing anyone at that time and here I was asking someone I didn't really know if they knew someone that might be interested in me. Well not straight out but I was young and horny what could I do.

The night we had set to meet, the bride did not even show up, she had sent a friend of hers. We had arranged another meeting and this time I met the bride to be and her friend, at first I just couldn't believe this was the bride. She was very nice to talk and laugh with but I couldn't get over the pins and rings in her lips and her eye brows. She was also very open with me, showing me the various pins and things, in other areas. It was strange as well to see someone at 8pm at night walking into the Denny's restaurant wearing sunglasses. I didn't think about it until later that night but man that was strange but cool. After the conservative hello's were given I sat down and started asking her what she wanted and what she thought she might like me to do for the ceremony. I have learned early on to make sure to ask the bride that. If nothing else happens ask her or the groom what they are looking for in the ceremony that way you can offer suggestions to help achieve that desired look. If they don't know, give them a small example of what you have done in the past with another wedding.

Anyway this is what I did, I gave her I believe about two or three examples of weddings that I have done in the past. Did she like them? Hell no, what she did do was take some bits from about five weddings that I ended up telling her about and putting them together. This was the time that the Celtic atmosphere was starting to really hit the United States again. So she wanted some Celtic things and other images in her wedding and I was more than happy to help her come up with some. I remembered being there for at least four hours when we finely left to go our separate ways, then she remembered about my question about someone I might like to go out with. I got the persons information from her and thanked her I left to go meet another friend that night for a late night film. It was not the same girl that the bride had sent to meet me that first night. I guess she was checking me out, or rather getting an approval before hand. I called the girl about two days later and we met at the same Denny's, which again I didn't think anything about until much later then I understood why we met there and why we met at that time. It was at this time, the vampires of Seattle had a meeting that was held at this Denny's and she wanted her friends to meet me. I think to make a decision about me, she might have been a wee bit off. But who would you believe was there, the bride to be.

At first I was a wee bit embarrassed but then I thought, what the hell. I then found out that night what I was finely expected to do at the wedding. I was to play wearing a cape of what I thought was really nice material and of course it was black. Also instead of the Scottish tuxedo or Prince Charlie coat that I normally wear, I was to wear this old style tuxedo made out of something that made me itch, my luck it was wool I think. Interesting but no I am still not sure what it was. My suggestion that if your client wants you to wear something of theirs make sure it fits, is wearable, and is not clashing with your kilt. In any case here, I am wearing this black cape with an old tuxedo and some type of boots that were a wee bit weird to wear playing the bagpipes in a kilt. Something else bothered me that night, the bride was thinking of having me wear fangs as well. The vampire is known because of its fangs of course and not kilts and tartan. My first thought was how in the hell was I going to play with fangs in my mouth. But I gave it try, why piss off the client too much, she might bite me. I tried playing them the next day it was a bit too weird. I ended up biting my lips many times but I soon got used to them. Things I do for women.

I then met the bride about three weeks later for the wedding rehearsal. When meeting with a wedding couple or a bride, I am hopeful that the bride had thought long enough before hiring me in thinking about tunes she wants. For this gives me enough time before the wedding to either learn any new tunes or at least practice old ones. Some tunes especially new ones tend to take me a while to learn. This one was no exception as the tune she wanted as the main tune was a bit complex and not the usual piping tune and at this point I don't even remember the name of the ones she wanted. That tells me that they weren't that important but the tune was strange and haunting.

At the rehearsal, I found out even more things that I didn't know I was going to be being doing for the ceremony. First off I was to go with the groom now to a secret meeting of vampires and meet his friends. It was like the bachelor party really but that night I was a wee bit nervous. Not from getting bit really but maybe getting something bad in the blood or some type of infection. You never know what to except. These friends of the groom asked me over and over to bite some girls they had there, and then drink what look like blood. I am sure it wasn't though, I hoped not anyway. Man was I nervous but at least I was friendly and not rude to them. I did have a few drinks and shots but that was it, or at least as far as I can remember. Remember, I wasn't going to be rude but I did nibble on a neck or two. I know I made a good impression on the groom who was laughing with me all the next day at the wedding telling his friends about things I guess I must have done. My wife likes to say I am a light weight when it comes to drinking and she must be right because I did not drink that much unless there was something else in the whiskey that I didn't know about. Oh well it was fun and at least I didn't bite anyone or get bitten and get some disease from them.

That night I also discovered that the bride was to bite some people during the wedding ceremony. This was going to be interesting but I knew I wasn't someone important to get bit or at least I hoped. However, that was not the case for I was chosen to be one of the bitten. The bride was a looker and was very nice person so too bad I guess I couldn't bite her back. Just because I didn't agree with the way she led her life didn't mean I had to be rude however I was really nervous about getting something. As a result when the bride did come over to me I politely informed her that I was sick however I did find out I was to be bit later and not at that time. She just nibbled my neck and no blood was drawn. Make up some good excuses when you need them and no harm will be done and it will keep you out of a touchy situation. Now that didn't stop the girl that was with me to bite me. So here I was dressed up and really ready to kill in this very strange outfit, playing the bagpipes with a girl that was dressed up in a black dress standing next to me the whole time waiting to bite me at any certain point in time. WOW!! That was the most nerve racking wedding I have preformed for yet. It left me twitching all night in order to protect my neck. Now as the ceremony progressed, I walked in the procession with the others of the wedding party to the front. The room that we were in was a club in downtown Seattle, the Catwalk. What an interesting place. A few years later it was the place to be when Bram Stoker's, 'Dracula' came out in the cinema. As I'm walking in the girl that had been standing with me, she informed me of some small changes, not to the wedding but afterwards. Oh boy, I thought here comes the really weird stuff. However, that was not the case, nothing too weird or so I was told. The bride and groom just wanted to meet me at their hotel and pay me my fee and have a drink. Ok I thought I could do that but as long as my blood wasn't the drink, ha ha.

As the ceremony continued, I stood up front with the wedding party and the same girl next to me when I felt something tugging my belt. I looked down and found the girl chaining herself to my belt. I gave her the "What the hell" look and she smiled and whispered "Not to worry". I smiled and thought, "oh god". When it came time for the biting part of the ceremony, I stood there while the girl next to me bit me, not hard but enough to make me bleed just a drop of two. It hurt and thank god I didn't get anything but it was bizarre. Then I was to play my next tune which I can't remember it maybe because I was light headed, but I remember that it was another dark tune. No da! After I was done the couple came forward over a bowl of water, or rather what I thought was water, giving their vows to each other. Then which I thought was even more out of the ordinary, they set the bowl on fire, it ended up being petrol fuel. It lit up the room and flamed for about half and hour or so. As I then played my next tune which was the main tune, I played for about two to three minutes and with the small room that we were in, I think that was enough. Just seeing the faces I could tell they wanted me to stop very soon as the echo was extensive.

At the end of the ceremony we walked out of the main room into the reception area. I continued to play for about another minute when the girl that was still chained to me nudged me to stop. I sat with her for the rest of the evening talking, laughing and having tons of drinks. They made punch that was deep red and I believed it was non alcoholic as I had a lot to drink with no effect, then some food that was both red and black in color. This couple made sure everything was right and suited the atmosphere of their wedding. It was stepping into a Halloween event that was just for the vampire in you. The lighting was dark but not too dark. All clothing of the wedding group was black some even wore leather but most wore black cloth. Even the staff of the club were dressed up to kill, literally. Chains were everywhere, leather trench coats, and people dressed like they were a French court, or an evil French court maybe. It was great and ended up being one wedding that I have never forgot.

Later that night I met up with the bride and groom at their hotel room, but instead of being the three of us they also had an entourage of girls and guys dressed up as vampires. The room was full of drinks, food and sex was going on everywhere. A huge orgy but with biting now being involved. They really wanted me to join in saying that I was a huge hit with everyone and many girls loved me in the kilt. Let's just say I was now scared shitless and didn't really know what to do. I'll leave it there and let you imagine what happened next.

At this next vampire sytle wedding, yes I did more then one, word got around. Anyway, I was asked to play for a girl that was a wee bit young I thought to even be engaged. I was to wear a leather kilt and a leather sleeveless shirt, at least the couple bought them for me as I couldn't have afforded it myself, at the time. Her husband to be asked me to walk her into the room that where they were getting married and just stand off to the side and play. What sounded fine to me ended up being an interesting night. But here I was standing there in my leather kilt and leather shirt, or jerkin when the bride came in. She was dressed up like a wee bit school girl at first I thought she was a guest so I didn't pay any attention to her or start playing. I didn't get a chance to talk or see her before hand, however I had known she was young. As she walked forward she came up beside me with a push telling me to play because the ceremony was starting. I looked down at her, she was holding a lollipop, short skirt with pigtails, and every guys dream as an innocent virgin. Although looking at her I though, WOW jail bate. I gave her a concerned look but then understood, so I started up my pipes and walked her into the room down a hallway. Now don't get me wrong I'm not condoning young marriages and I didn't play for this wedding for the money. I almost did it for free, its just I thought it would be an interesting thing to do and actually I didn't know how young she was until latter.

So I'm walking her into the room, which because we didn't have a chance to do a rehearsal I received a large shock, for as I walked in as there was an altar with three people standing in robes behind it. At first I thought some type of sheep but it turned out to be a plush toy. Thank god! Then I wondered who was to actually be sacrificed.

They started the ceremony and the groom was dressed up like a teacher, hated the irony in this wedding, however they did get married by doing did all the usual wedding vows. During the ceremony it got really interesting with a gothic flare to it by killing that poor sheep and pretending to drink its blood which was red wine, or so I hoped. So no actual person or animal was sacrificed. Now even though all this is going on to my amazed eyes, I couldn't leave the room as that would have been rude or even scary in case they came after me. When it was over the couple came over, asked me if I wanted to go to the reception. I declined more because I had another wedding to do later that day but also because I was unsure of where the rest of the evening events were heading especailly after the last wedding. The other wedding was true, really but I was also very nervous about what they were thinking of doing. I can only imagine but I talked with them later that week and did find out that she was younger than the groom 15 vs. 25 years old. I couldn't believe it, but they told me the wedding was just a practice and they were going to get married for real in two to three years but really wanted to imagine what it would be like. Oh boy! What an imagination!

As you know, I have a love for vampires and things of that nature, so after doing that one vampire wedding I guess I was in a trance and wanted to do something else. Well a few months later I got that opportunity and was asked to drive to Vancouver B.C. where a group that does vampire events was holding a vampire ball of some kind. Canada is such a great country to visit and would love to stay too, but thats another story. Turned out that one of the guests at the wedding was the coordinator of this event and was impressed that I was a piper that liked to have fun. He told me that a lot of Canadian pipers don't like to do things like this. Don't know if thats true or not, didn't care really as I was having fun, their loss I thought. However, turned out what should have been a fun night ended up me being in jail and almost kicked out of the country. Saturday night came and I dressed up in my finest as I wore my kilt along with my Prince Charlie jacket and a red sash, that looked good for a vampire event I thought. When I came around the corner and saw right off that I was over dressed. Now everyone was dressed well, but much like vampires would wear, you can let your imagination take over, not a tux in site though. The coordinator saw me and pulled me inside to tell me that I was to just walk in the first couple of people, that had won a contest, down the hall into the dance room where the party was. Easy I thought!

When it came time I was ready as I could be and proceeded to walk the 3 couples down the hall and into the dance room. After that I was asked just to look good and enjoy the rest of the night. With my room paid for and food I was going to have a good time, I thought no matter what. The whole event didn't even start until 9pm and it didn't take the audience a lot of time to get into things. They had drinks, red wine of course, food, all red and made to look bloody. Even had some wee bit people to look like dwarves I guess walking around giving entertainment. It was fun watching people really, until I came around the corner into a dark room. At this point I thought, oh yep this is a vampire party alright for here were more people doing S&M and other things that you can only imagine. Now I thought, well I can hear it now or read it in the newspaper, "A bagpiper was arrested in a S&M party downtown that was raided." It did happen to my total surprise, I was at the bar having a drink having a talk with a young something when police came in and started breaking the party up. They were really very nice to me, for they were making fun of the many unusual people at this event, as they took me and threw me into a car and drove downtown. I guess they thought I was at least some what normal, even wearing a kilt. I spent a few hours in the jail explaining that I was just hired to play the pipes and nothing else. Turned out that many of the people there were doing drugs, both selling and buying and let's say interesting things that were illegal. They let me go with no problems but asked that I go home, which I did. I got to the hotel hoping for a nights sleep but it was 5am then, what a waste I thought.

That morning as I went back through the border I was asked by the guard to drive to the side and go through a security check. I had no problem with that for it made me feel that they were doing their job. I pulled off to the side and walked in the building where as a few guards went through my car, I showed them my passport and information. When one of the guards came in carrying my pipe case I didn't think anything about it until he flopped it on top of the table in front of me. Then it hit me, the police in the city might have put information out about what happened the night before and I bet my name was in there. "So whats in here?" the guard asked. I told him a musical instrument and then I was asked to open it up. I did slowly thinking of course back to when I did that at the airport. At least here they knew what it was or least I hoped so for who knows I thought with American border guards. They looked through the case finding nothing then telling me to have a good day. I was shocked and surprised too so I thanked them and drove away as fast as I could. That's the last time I ever played for an abnormal event like that, though not my last off the wall one, though I do miss those types of events with people who don't care what others think of them and that are just out to have an unusual and fun time.

Now this one is not a wedding or event but something very out of the ordinary that happened to me. New Year's Day 1996 I was working as a manager in a place that had dancers. Well yes it was female dancers, not my best job in the world but the money was good and I enjoyed it, not because I saw nude women each day, well maybe but I did enjoy the job.

I was asked by a few of the girls to come to their place and join in the New Years party that they were holding. I knew a few of the girls and believe it or not they were very nice girls, well I thought they were as they paid me very well each night for protecting them from some of the customers that we got. They asked if I could play so when the bell tolled midnight I would play some good tunes to get the mood going. I never got to midnight.

As the night wore on I sat off to the side wearing my kilt laughing and having a good time with the girls and friends that were at the house when 2 of the girls asked if I wanted a drink, of course so I walked up to the bar and talking to another as she made the drink. They handed it to me and that is the last I remember. They told me later with pictures, which I hope are burnt now because it is still a little embarrassing, I took the drink, then fell to my knees and passed out. I don't know how long I stayed like that but when I woke up people were cheering the new year and didn't seem to care about me as I crawled outside to throw up in the bushes. At least I thought later I was nice to them and not getting sick in their house.

I threw up and then when I felt better called a taxi and left the party. I got home and passed out that night waking up the next morning with the worst headache a person could probably imagine. I walked out and into the kitchen where my mum who was visiting was sitting having her breakfast. She looked up smiling but instantly screamed when she saw me of course giving me another headache. I sat down holding my head trying to understand what she was saying until she passed out herself. When I was leaning down that was when I found out what she was screaming about as a drop of blood fell onto her face.

I jumped up and went over to the nearest mirror and saw my face, swollen eyes and tired looking but it was the blood coming out of my eyes that made me freak out. I ran over to the phone and called the medic's who came a while later to find me sitting on the sofa holding my head. The man checked my mum as the woman came over to me, instantly going into a panic and taking me down to the ambulance where they took me to the hospital. Where I was giving enough meds to survive the day and more. Turned out that somehow the drugsthe girls had given me what ever they were had done something to me and when I had thrown up it had caused my eyes blood vessels to blow up inside my eyes.

A few days later when I felt well I went back to work. That's when the fun began for me. During the night working in the dark rooms, that was the dance building, I walked around making sure the girls were doing the right things and nothing illegal was going on, if you know what I mean. I didn't know it until one of the girls told me that when I stood under a black light my eyes glowed. "Really?" I said and walked over to a dark corner I knew had a black light above it and sat there. I ended up scaring the girls and even many customers who later would tell me that all they saw was 2 glowing eyes watching them. I took advantage of it and used it to scare people for a few days, you can imagine the sight it must have been, a guy comes in to enjoy himself and there while he's sitting in the dark looks over and sees 2 glowing eyes watching him instead.

NUDE WHAT?

Inever in my life thought I would ever do a wedding at a nudist camp but it happened to me as well. One thing leads to another and before you know it your asked to do some of the oddest and most interesting things using the bagpipes, and this one was an odd one for me, a nudist wedding. This was a total first for me but at least I got paid for it. It happened really after I was asked by a local rock radio station in Seattle to play the pipes for a party that they were holding at the local nudist camp which was strange in itself. It was astonishing to think of doing something like that however I thought what the hell, especially after the DJ's had me come into the station and talk to some of the people from the camp. Of course going live over the radio and speaking about the upcoming event kind of goated me into it. This convinced me to come out, well sort of. In all actuality, I really think it was the girls that were in the station, getting the idea in my head that they would be there. At first I had no intention of going to play in the nude, although when I got out there things changed. For they had security which of course were in the nude, making sure people were nude after they left a building meant for people to shead their clothes in. As a result of changing or rather sheading my clothes, I told them that this was my first time, a virgin nudist is what they called me. I walked out of the changing room but then ran back in with embarrassment. I asked if I could wear something, they said as long as I was nude in the back end it was not a problem so I grabbed my sporran. At least I would have something covering me up, he he. I went over to the DJ's booth and yes they were both in nothing but their headsets and I got everything ready to play. I warmed up behind the main tent and had a few drinks, water of course! However something stronger would have been helpful at that moment. The whole event was a lot more fun then I had thought and not the least bit embarrassing. At the end a helicopter came out and took a picture of all of the people there laying on the ground or standing making out the letters of the radio station. From that I ended up getting asked to do a wedding and at the same place in the near future! The most interesting thing for me was, I got a tan in the most interesting places.

This wedding was hilarious to be in but also bizarre because I had never been to a nudist camp, other than the party mentioned before, not even a nude beach in my life. Wait that is wrong I've been to one in France, but I was there for fun not work and I was not the one dressed up or rather dressed down. In the end I guess it was the money and maybe the chance to say I've been in a nudist wedding.

Well doing a wedding and the radio event was something else. This one was going to be on a sunny day at least, thank god I thought I couldn't imagine doing a nudist event in the cold or rain. The people at the camp were pretty fascinating people to talk with and see, he he. I of course was playing the bagpipes and was the only entertainment which I found out once I arrived at the event itself. So I asked what I was expected to do. I always remembered to find out as soon as possible on what your position is in the wedding or ceremony because you might find you're in an awkward place in the end, for the pipes do not always allow for cramped spots not just because of the sound but the size of this instrument. Not that I was in an awkward place, I just was feeling odd because I was doing something new. I was to walk the bride up the walkway and then to the altar, or what they had as an altar. The priest, the bride's maid, the groomsman, and the parents of the bride were all going to be nude. That was thrilling, and scary, seeing people who didn't take care of themselves for years, health wise that is, as well as seeing beauties fully nude. Great stuff!

So here was a priest only dressed in a collar, bride's maid with only the flowers, groomsmen dressed only with ties and parents wearing nothing. The groom of course was wearing a black bow tie but the bride was wearing her veil and makeup, that is it. The weather was great. We had so much fun doing the wedding and seeing all of the people that can either scare you or make you want to join up. I walked in the bride trying to concentrate on my playing but it was very hard not to look here and there because many, and I mean many were nude but not all. Some scared me and others... well you get the picture. I got up to the front and played until I knew when to stop, stepping off to the side I waited while the ceremony got on. Here I was just wearing my sporran covering the important things and carrying my pipes. At least it was sunny and warm, I kept thinking which kept my mind focused so I did not get embarrassed and run away. Standing up there with eyes all over me which I felt followed my every move while trying not to look at the people. I did notice a few girls and one or two guys giving that wink or nod to me. I'd nod back or smile to the girls but it was a wee bit nerve racking for me. No guys sorry I don't go that way. The gay weddings are in another chapter and that is another story.

The wedding got over in about half an hour and I then walked the couple out, playing a wonderful tune. However, on the walk out I received a number of pinches, even one pinch that was very hard which gave me a bruise that lasted for at least a week. I took the couple to this building where they got changed which I don't know why, but they did. The rest of the people just walked over to the pool and food area and started drinking and eating. I stayed for about half an hour, oh ok truthfully an hour talking to a few people flirting and being flirted with. I never did see the wedding couple again so they must have taken off. I guess the great thing about that wedding is that I received two party invitations from it, one from an older woman who was retiring from a job in Vancouver, Canada. The other was for a young woman who wanted someone to play the bagpipes at her bridal hen party. I'll go over that party first.

Even though I met the bride to be at the nudist

wedding and I played at the bridal party nevertheless I didn't play in the nude for this event. It turned out to be a laugh for the two of us and we both had fun, or at least I did. Her bridal party was a closed party at the Hilton in Vancouver Canada. Very nice place to see and stay at too, I made the point to remember to stay there some time in the future. The bride wanted me to walk her in and just stand off to the side and play for a few minutes. Doesn't sound peculiar right? Well that was the normal part of the party, it's what happened afterwards that becomes a bit of a shock. You've heard of how women all think that men in kilts are one of the sexist things ever? Well this is where I really found out how sexy they really think it is. The bride or someone had ordered to have some male strippers come and do a show for them. Normal stuff for a bachelorette party right? For women I guess it is, but here I was playing the pipes for guess who? Two guys wearing tiny kilts, it looked like they were women's dresses, to begin with anyway. After a while I couldn't play anymore as my lips were tired, so I stopped and put my pipes down where they could be safe and walked over to get something to drink at the bar. The bride didn't care that I had stopped she was having too much fun watching something else. I wonder what?

Here is where I personally thought it got weird for me. This of course is not a sexual story that I've written, though this might have happened to you if you wore a kilt. I was over at the bar trying not to watch the dancing by the guys, not my scene, that was going on when two ladies who were probably around 18-25 years old and of course were so drunk that they started to hit on me. Well I was very uncomfortable because I was working and trying to be discreet and not seen, as these other guys were flashing and dancing around the room nude. However, these were very nice looking women that had come up to me. They thought I guess I was part of the show even though they had seen me playing for a while earlier. This room we were in was very big and I had played on the deck of the place so it wasn't loud inside but I'm sure these girls knew I was there since the beginning you know what I mean. Here they were groping me and trying to get up my kilt. Let's just say for those that know the life of wearing a kilt, I did get a phone numbers from them, though I was still a professional in the end I kissed them on the cheeks. The bride was very happy with my playing and how I handled her guests she and I have remained friends for many years. Years afterwards I was nervous talking to her in case she really did know about the girls that I received the phone numbers from. I never did call them. I did find out a few years after that she was the one that told the girls to come over to me. She knew that I was single and looking, so....

BEAM ME UP?

Now these themes are a favorite of mine to do. Why, well I guess it's because down deep somewhere inside me I'm a sci-fi nerd. Or at least that is what my wife says I am as does my neighbors, family, the butcher, the news agent...anyway. I love anything to do with space and other planets and being that I don't think I'll ever get to one in my lifetime I might as well dream about them, you know. Therefore when I was asked by some people to do a science fiction setting of a wedding I took the opporunity to have some fun. Wee Bit did I know that it would involve Klingons, Vulcan's and many other aliens that we today find in sci-fi movies, shows and more.

The first one I did was while I was living in Boston, Massachusetts. A beautiful city though very hot and humid during the summer. I was with some friends doing the annual St. Patrick's celebrations there in the city when I was asked by another friend if I had the time that particular weekend to do a small wedding near the city centre. To top it off it was a science fiction type wedding. The bride was to be a Vulcan, I heard and the groom was something out of Battlestar Galactica or Star Wars. I was excited in the end and here was my chance to see something either that was going to be amusing, or at least something attention grabbing. What I got was both.

I met the groom later that day at a pub in Dorset, a small suburb south of downtown Boston. We talked for about two hours, I believe just having a good time getting to know each other. His bride called him a few times, I remembered it being at least 3-4 times, however we talked about what he wanted and what it would be time wise. They wanted me to stand off to the side and play something very haunting. Playing this instrument, well that would be no problem, as many tunes are haunting anyway. It gave me the thought however, that this was something else other than a sci-fi wedding and that something else was going on.

The bride would walk in and sing a song, which I was told was something that Klingons do in Star Trek. I had to take his word at that I didn't know. I like sci-fi but I'm not up on every wee bit thing when it comes to all the complex stories that are in the sci-fi world. After the bride to be sang, she would walk over near me while I was playing then I would complete her walk down the aisle, with me escorting her to where the groom was going to be standing. The groom would then sing a song as well. The surprise feature of this wedding was it was right after a Star Trek: The Next Generation had started on television and they wanted to add some things that were in the show to the ceremony at the last minute. My luck it would be some wedding where everyone would be nude however that was not the case. The guests had dressed like all sorts of aliens and even some people I couldn't even imagine what they were. And here I was, dressed in a kilt, with a Prince Charlie tuxedo, a wee bit out of place I thought, however I was given a sash that they said was used in a Star Trek show from the 1960's. Interesting I thought, ok, so now I was wearing this sash that was bright green with gold trim in addition to playing some haunting tunes, and tunes that usually come to mind when playing a funeral however this is what the wedding couple wanted. I couldn't remember exactly what those tunes were today, but they were something like 'Mist Covered Mountains' or 'Skye Boat Song'. It was then that it got even more interesting during this wedding, or weird I guess however you want to look at it. Two people walked out and fought a sword battle like in Star Wars, but a wee bit more dramatic and right in front of the wedding couple before they started to exchange vows. The actors gasped, and grunted while they fought, some in the audience were laughing, I think. Then some others walked out and sung here and there, it was interesting to say the least. Not much happened after that, if that wasn't enough.

Fantasy weddings I find are different from anything else for they go in all different directions at once. They are a bunch of people that are playing characters from books, films or just ones imagination. Within the last few years Lord of the Rings has had a huge influence on fantasy weddings and events. I did go to an event in 2003 when I saw people dressed up in Star Trek, Babylon

5, Lord of the Rings, and even Red Dwarf costumes. At this event I was playing for a huge occurrence that took place in Seattle, Washington where many actors and people got together to just celebrate, what it was I had no idea. However it was all centered on a coronation of some kind with a plot and some kind of assassination, very theatrical. It is fun watching people walk around dressed up, but it is funnier to watch people act like they know what they are doing. A vampire dressed like a Star Trek officer or a Star Wars storm trooper talking like they are from Vulcan. Ok yes, I am a bit of a geek when it comes to this but not only the history but the movies. I ended up being asked by another couple that were getting married the next year to come back and play for them. They promised me it was a fantasy themed wedding, but it would be normal. What's normal I thought. And they said that I could bring my girlfriend, at the time and now my wife, if I wanted too. So of course I did bring her, I think she had more fun than I did.

Nothing weird really happened at this wedding, the normal things you would see, Vulcans, tons of Darth Vaders, who all seemed to want to fight each other. Many Trekkies, elves with light sabers, that sort of stuff. I played for the wedding, but right after it my wife who was hiding by now because she was getting afraid of these people ran over to me and pulled me out of the building and made me drive her home. Since then she has told me please never take her to one of these types of weddings, it totally fricked her out. I dragged my wife through not only conventions such as this but through many battle fields and even one on our honeymoon, Hastings in England. My bagpipe playing was fun to hear at this event, however and the responses from these people were like it was a thing from another planet or something that they had never heard.

ZORRO THE GAY BLADE

For me to do a gay wedding or event was a very panicky feeling for me at first. I'm not a person that disagrees with that way of life or even has a problem with it. It's just something that I can't understand even though I have many friends around the world that are gay and are vast more fun to be around because of the great attitude they have on life. I've even been told I act gay, why, maybe it's the kilt? I hope so. Doing parties and weddings for them I can say are some of the most colorful and interesting of all the events that I have done over the years. Why? Well I really couldn't really say, but I end up having a really good time laughing and more.

The first event that I did was just a party from what I was told anyway. The party was at the local rugby clubhouse because this person was a player in the club. I arrived in plenty of time and my only job was to walk in with the birthday cake, pretty much like walking the haggis in on Burn's Night, however I should have suspected something at this point. Of course being my first event of this type, I was a bit naive. I walked into the club and was amazed at the décor that was there. It didn't have things saying "Happy Birthday" or "Good job mate". No not things like that. There were signs saying things like, "Coming out" and "Finely mate", not that it bothered me or actually that I thought much of it at the time as I had to get ready. I walked over to a spot and started to put my pipe box down when a gentleman came over and introduced himself as the main player's best friend. That was how he introduced himself. We talked for about two – three minutes and I went into a small room where I could warm up my pipes and get ready for fun. About 20 minutes later people started to arrive, but not the main person. I sat in the back trying not to be seen, but I watched the people coming in. This I didn't think would be a normal party as these people were dressed up like it was a party in New Orleans or Italy at Carnivale, and I also noticed that there were no women in this party.

The time came for me to play for the cake while I was really starting to wonder about the guests at this party and then finally I saw the person the party was for. He came in laughing, joking and thanking people, however as he took off his jacket, he was only wearing a kilt and a short one at that. Oh boy! Then I saw the cake come out from another room, it was a bit on the large size, I thought. Large, I guess would make that cake sound small, because it was huge, enormous really. I did my job and played the cake in to the main celebration area. When I arrived at the front where the guest of honor was sitting and walked off to the side to finish my tune, the cake exploded and a guy came out dancing to my playing. I was a bit shocked and hesitated for a second or two however the dancer indicated to me to keep playing, so I did, trying not to laugh. I had to turn a wee bit so I couldn't see the guy's willy bouncing all over the place.

I've been told that I'm a wee bit slow or ignorant in things about life sometimes or have been in the past. It really took me a few minutes to finely figure out what was going on before the cake came out. It wasn't the poster or décor that was hanging about, but the people themselves. Oh! Was my first thought, ok, I think I need to leave now! So when I was done playing I tried to make a quick escape to the back to get my pipe box, but I was stopped by a guy who offered me a drink to thank me for playing. It is tradition to pay the piper with Scotch as well. He asked me to stay but I said I really had to go, but didn't want to be rude so I had the one drink. I was there for at least another hour. What a day I thought when I got home!

This led to another party for me, but this time it was a bachelor party for the groom, or bride, I really couldn't tell when I arrived what the nature of the couple was. It was another simple job, just playing or so I was told when the groom/bride showed up and play for a few minutes outside. It turned out that the party would have dancers as well, I guess as entertainment. Pretty easy I thought, so I started to warm up and get ready. Parties like these were easy to do, not much to practice for unlike weddings which usually had special requests. I was warming up and watching people walk in when I noticed the clothes the guests were wearing, much like the previous party however with a bit more class or unclass I guess would be the right world. I was trying not to laugh at some of them. Then the dancers showed up, which led to even more confusion as they thought I was part of the entertainment as well. They had been told that a musician was going to be there to play for them. I was very surprised at this. We discussed the particulars and decided that they just needed something played to get them in and up on stage, sounded simple enough, as long as I didn't have to watch. So I did my part, walking in the groom/bride, still didn't ask who was who, and played for about 2 minutes outside. Then came the really interesting part as these three dancers came in dressed up as the Village People. I stood off to the side of the stage and played while they walked in and up to the stage. I was so embarrassed by this, not what I had expected at all. To make it even more distressing for me as I waited to wrap things up, get paid, a guy who must have thought I was gay I guess started to hit on me and would not take no for an answer. It took the staff and the groom/bride to get him off me because he was very drunk. So here was this guy being dragged off screaming at me saying that I was the love of his life. The groom/bride came up later and apologized for his friend and gave me an extra big tip in helping out by playing for the dancers when their own musician didn't show up, which explained a few things.

Now over the years as I have travelled and performed, I have made many friends that are gay, however the previous two events awkwardness was due to the sequence of events but let me to a one good friend in

Seattle, who is a minister and a counsellor for couples. Being Irish and gay has allowed him to always be a great laugh and he holds a great heart. We have ended up doing at least 20-30 weddings together before I left Seattle in 2004. We also did a few smaller events as well, such as naming celebrations, birthdays and so much more. Working with him I felt that my humor and his were such a great match that we could get away with almost anything, which we did here and there. To give you an idea of his sense of humor, one wedding that we did together. He was standing up in front of the guests, since he was the minister, this made since. While we waited for the couple to come out, he asked the guests to help with a game to be played on the wedding couple during the ceremony, which I will get to in a second. There were many guest that took up the challenge.

I piped them in and stood in my normal spot behind the bride's maids, as he started to introduce the couple and talk about the rules and such of being married when he finely stopped. He then instead of asking are there any objections, asked is there was anyone in the audience that wanted to say goodbye to the groom. A few people got up, but most were older women and men. Then a young girl got up and said goodbye. The bride gave the groom a look like, "What the hell?" The groom just gave a nervous smile like, "I don't know, honest?" Then a few more got up and said goodbye. Finally, a man that the groom I guess worked with stood up and said goodbye, saying that he would miss the groom and the summer fling had been fun while it lasted. The minister had prearranged everyone to do this of course. The laughter was deafening after that because the bride was getting a wee bit mad, turning a red too if I remember, and gave the groom a wee bit nudge. However, this is the point the minister turned the tables and asks if there is anyone who wants to say good-bye to the bride, which led to further laughter. Now knowing this friend the way I do he makes sure that the couple is good natured and able to handle something like this which they both ended up laughing with the guests.

Things like this were just a wee bit taste of his weddings. When one day he and I were to do another wedding together we just made sure that the couple was going to have a good time. The two of us together, oh what a wedding!

I was to play the pipes as normal walking in the bride at the beginning of the wedding. The groom was of course already there. Sean, the minister's humorist way decided to talk about the rules of being married,when both he and I played a joke on the groom. I walked out and grabbed his hand and said sorry for not asking him earlier for his hand in marriage. The bride was furious at first like they usually are, but in the end she took it quite well. Oh I love weddings.

Now back to another gay wedding, I was asked to do was with two girls that wanted to get married on a boat in Seattle's Lake Union. The boat was an old ferry boat that was used in the early 20th century and now is being used as a reception, party type boat, and by the way is the same boat that my wife and I happened to have met on a few years earlier. Wee Bit thing this boat, so with a lot of people on it, the weddings could get, let's say crowded! This couple who was celebrating a joining were wonderful to work with not only that they worked for a local fire department in Seattle which surprised me when I found out. No problems with this really but I can say that I'd want them to save me if I had problems, as they were also buff as hell. Somewhere in their personalities they good natured and easy going attitude which later led to the relaxed and friendly environment of a wedding. Sean was ministering this wedding as well. I got together with one of the couple didn't know which one she was going to be and went over the plans. She was great to talk with and had a really good idea off what they wanted. So I get to the boat on the wedding day wearing my kilt of course, the weather was great, sun coming down over the water behind us, with a huge amount of people on the bow of the boat, giving me the feeling that the boat might tip over for a while. However after I walked them in for the ceremony, I started to notice the guests of the couple. I felt like I was in an episode of Rocky Horror Picture Show, the costumes were let's say, interesting?

During the reception which took place in the back and middle of the boat, I was talking to one of the guests when a young lad came to me and asked me if I was up for a dance. I really wasn't and declined. He was cool with it but a few minutes later I guess his boyfriend came up to me and gave me a mouthful, oh sorry about the pun, about talking to his boyfriend. I didn't know who he was he just came up to me! However since my wife had also attended this wedding she was able to cool things down by coming over and touching my arm with her wedding band hand. He promptly apologized however we left shortly after that. Oh what a day. From that wedding I was asked to do three more weddings within the next year. Some were fellow firefighters and some weren't but got to love how people talk.

The next event was an engagement party that I did that included a gay couple that were close friends of mine, both of the girls that would be getting married had been together for over 10 years, although I hadn't known them quite that long. With all the laws that said that they couldn't marry officially but they just couldn't wait. I was just an added gift to them by the time they decided to do an actual ceremony, they so enjoyed the playing of the bagpipes that my playing was a gift for the celebration. Nevertheless they decided to add a wee bit fun and games as their ceremony was the day before my birthday.

Now in the America most people don't know the tradition of Bonfire Night, some knew that it was an important day in Britain. They decided to have their celebration or rather engagement party at the local British pub in Seattle which I found out later was on my behalf, including the fireworks, singing, food and everything that they arranged to make it a fun night. Since the party was closer to a wedding ceremony celebration then an actual engagement party we just ended up having fun, but since they couldn't get married for real it was just a party for everyone who might have come in. My part in this wee bit party was just to walk out and play in the corner and provide some music while people showed up. Easy and that's what I did. I played for about 15 or so minutes with everyone showing up and having a good laugh thinking it was a wedding finding it just a total party. When I was done I walked over to a chair and had a drink of water. I found out year earlier that when I'm done playing I've always been thirsty and have been known to drink two to three bottles of water when I am finished.

So here I was drinking a bottle of water when the couple came up and thanked me and gave me a gift on top of the fact that the celebration included so many English favorites. Now this is just after I met my future wife, only two months before and yes we were engaged and getting everything ready to marry. Nevertheless their gift was something that was hard to say no too. A girl! They knew that I had a great sense of humor but didn't know or just forgot that I was engaged, now. Consequently, it was very embarrassing for me to say no and at first I had trouble, so I had a few drinks with her and got to know her. Of course, in the end I had to say no, nevertheless she was so sweet and cute. She was a close friend of the couple and I'd met her before. She told me that she had inquired about me to them, so that's how we ended up meeting that day. Happy days I guess!

CELEBRATE!!

I didn't really want to go over all the people that I've played for that were famous or are or were celebrities however I was advised to at least input a few that are some highlights of my life. Being a bagpipe player and playing for the queen, which I have talked about, is of course the highest honor however after that and other key memorable events that I mentioned earlier playing for some great actors of our time has been tremendous as well.

The first of which comes to mind is playing for the actor, Sir Sean Connery. It was a birthday party and he had come to Edinburgh from Spain to meet some friends. I was asked to come and play something normal but unusual for him and of course I was more than happy to do that. After playing my wee bit I walked over to say happy birthday to the man, it turned out that he was totally different then some people had said. He was very nice, he and I shared a glass of port together and talked about football and music. It was a great night and I just wished I had gotten his signature, but I did years later when a friend of mine in Los Angeles who works in the

Hollywood business gave me a picture of Sean doing an advert for the Austin Martin car that he used in a Bond film.

The next actor that I can say hit me right off was Richard Karn from the "Home Improvement" show in America. It was while I was the golf course piper in Newcastle, Washington and his father was celebrating his birthday. I didn't even know it was for Richard's father until I walked in the room playing 'Scotland the Brave', and I turned around and saw Richard sitting there with a huge grin on his face. It was great and both where loving it. After I got done I congratulated the birthday boy and shook hands with Richard and he told me he'd come downstairs to thank me with a drink. I walked downstairs to the clubhouse pub and waited and waited. Well he never showed up but it was great to meet him, being that at that time he was on my favorite TV show. He was a very nice gentleman to meet.

When I was in New England, I had a chance to play for someone from Professional Wrestling which was big in the late 80's. The star of the show was Roddy 'Rowdy' Piper who by the way is a bagpiper himself though more into his profession of wrestling. Roddy was a great guy to meet. At that time sweaty, full of insults, ready to kill his opponent and huge. I was still having fun. Being that his character was Scottish, Roddy had pipers walk him in from the back to the front stage. His regular piper was sick that night which I can't understand why, too much fun! So I was called in to play and had a few laughs with him before walking Roddy down the aisle to the stage where he won the night's matches against is opponents. It was a great night for me as well, I got paid very well and I got to see how fake the wrestling that we see on TV was. Oh, I don't think I was supposed to say that! Sorry Roddy, you're still great though!

Now while living in Seattle I had many chances to meet, play and have great times with some of the movie, sports and music stars, thanks much to my wife's marketing skills. Even though I'm not an American sports fan and never could understand some of their games, I was a fan of some of the players. Why, well they were very nice people, plus it was great that many of them use their time to support kids around the city, as well as be someone they can look up to. So when I was asked to play at a wedding of an agent that took care of many sports players in the city of Seattle, it was my pleasure thinking maybe I could meet some of them!

The wedding was going to be at this new hotel in Kirkland, a suburb of Seattle, and the hotel was right on the water of Lake Washington, the biggest lake in Washington State. This took place unfortunately two days after 9/11 so a lot of the guests that were supposed to be there, couldn't make it in. The agent was the groom and the bride to be worked for the FBI. Even though I wasn't supposed to know but having military training in spotting certain people, got to love the British army for that, I knew something was up with her. It was a normal wedding nothing extraordinary except we had a few moments to say a few prayers for the people in New York City. The unique thing about this wedding however was the people my wife and I had a chance to meet for we sat at a table that had a few important people including a hockey player from the Seattle Thunderbirds. He and I talked about the game and life. During the reception I got to talk to Gary Paden of the Seattle Sonics the basketball team there at that time. The really funny thing was he had never seen a set of bagpipes before so I gave him a try at it. It was great fun and here I was talking to him having some great laughs and pictures together while he is playing my pipes, or rather trying to, they do take a lot of hot air to play. A few other sports stars were there including American football players from the Seattle Seahawks and the Tacoma baseball teams. I had a fun night but when some of the guests' beepers went off everyone knew that something was up and they left rather suddenly. The bride had to catch a lift back to Washington DC by catching a military flight out of the airbase south of Seattle. I never did find out exactly what was up however I was able to ascertain that the group the bride worked with was working at the Pentagon and they needed her fast.

Of all the celebrities I guess I can say that I've met the one person that I can say made me feel like I was doing something for a reason, was Princess Diana. When I met her I was attached to the Black Watch 1st Battalion where I was a medic. She came by with Prince Charles to check out some of the military a surprise inspection of a sort. I, with the rest of the pipers of the battalion played for them and then stood in attention while they walked the line as I later called it. When she came to me she asked me about two – three questions. It was so hard for me to answer mainly because I was over struck by her beauty. I couldn't believe how beautiful she was. It was a great day for me. When she died I was in Seattle at the time and had the chance to sign a book of condolences at the local British consulate, while there I ended up talking to the consulate general. For this reason I ended up playing for the British consulate general for some very special events for politicians that came over from England to do business with Boeing, or Microsoft. It was with much exhilaration and enthusiasm that I was able to do many events at the consulates house near Lake Washington.

BLIND FAITH IN HER

When I met my wife I had just left the US army with the wonderful gift of PTSD. I wasn't feeling at my best when I was asked by a young lady to play for her wedding on this old ferry boat in Seattle. She was a lovely girl and Irish all the way, Irish name, red hair and anger that matches the image of a perfect Irish girl. This and so much more made her fun to work with because on the day of the rehearsal she changed my life forever. My part in their ceremony was done for a while just walking them in about ten minutes prior and being a bit wee bored I was standing off to the side of the pier while she and her husband to be were going over their vows. The bride saw me there, just leaning against the wall so she came over when her part was done to talk to me. We got to know each other pretty well in that fifteen minute conversation. Laughing about life and such, she asked me the question that I believe is taught to all girls in school, "Are you seeing anyone?" When I answered no, "Well I might know someone that you might like!" I thanked her and said sure why not. Since I am not one that received the James Bond looks or achieve the attitude I have always had problems attracting girls, well kind of. But I thought what the hell! Later at the rehearsal dinner I met more of her family which consisted of a barbeque and a whole lot of food. It was great.

The next day I got dressed in my Prince Charlie Tuxedo got my pipes tuned up and showed up about half an hour before the wedding was to start. I talked to the bride and groom and made sure nothing had changed for at times things do at the last minute. Nothing was changed so I went up stairs to the command deck and got my pipes ready. I had 20 or so minutes before people would start showing up. Being on the command deck I was able to see over the gang plank where the guests would walk on board, a perfect opportunity to check the girls out, ha ha!

I was pretty much ready with pipes tunes up, they were hot and good to go, when I saw a young lady and what looked like her mother walk from the car park to the boat. From where I was she was wearing a black or dark dress that was low cut. Long reddish-brown hair and a great figure, someone I thought, was too pretty for me to even have a chance at. Oh did I forget to tell you, I had asked a girl out after the rehearsal dinner and gone out with her for a bite to eat after that, even asked her to attend the wedding the next day with me. The bride said it was ok to bring her along, which I did. The only problem was I thought she was nice but not really my type, but at least I had someone there to talk too. I've always been a romantic person believing in fate that some day I would find someone even if she was a sheep, she would be my soul mate. I was not meant to die alone and I had faith that I would know her when she came a long.

The bride came up to the command deck and I stood with her getting ready. She was nervous but in good cheer and laughing with her bridesmaids. "Here we go, down and into the future of hell",she said. Interesting saying, I thought!

I started playing and we walked down the stairs. I was nervous at this wedding that I'd trip and fall down breaking not only my neck but my pipes as well, due to the steepness of the stairs on the boat so I took it really slow. Plus tripping the bride on the way down would not have been pleasant. When we got to the bottom of the stairs I took the bride out to the aft of the boat where the ceremony would take place under an archway that had been erected with the skyline of Seattle behind it. Not a big area, but had a nice background. I walked up front and stood off to one side in my normal place next to the bridesmaids. There I looked over the crowd and there I saw the girl that I saw from the command deck and she smiled at me. Oh boy I thought, this is interesting as I looked at her she took my breath away. Nevertheless I stood my ground and made sure that my job was done right.

When the ceremony itself ended I started up and walked the new couple off the aft deck and into the reception area which is where if you were a car you would be sitting. The deck was brooking up into two sections. On one side was the bar and dance floor, the other side were where the tables and food were. When people finished eating, of course people went to the other side and started to dance. For some reason I can't remember why I didn't stand next to the girl I brought not very gentlemen like, sorry. But here I was standing there off to the side of the dance floor watching people dance, and many people drink remember, Irish Wedding! Coming out of the crowd and not hard to miss was the bride. She thanked me for making the day special. She had a great time and asked if I was still open to meeting the person she was thinking about, I said yes, no problem, hoping that the other girl might not notice.

The bride disappeared and came back with a girl in her hand. I couldn't believe it, it was the girl I noticed from the command deck and the one who had smiled at me when I was standing on the aft deck. It was her and my knees got a wee bit weak. Calm down mate your doing fine I told myself. The bride came up and introduced her as her cousin and then ran off hoping that we would talk which we did of course. Small talk at first but she took my arm as we walked around the deck. We talked for at least half an hour before I realized that I was having a good time with this girl and I should really ask her out. She went to excuse herself claiming to have to check on her mother which is when I got her number. As she left, I made my way over to the girl I had come with however she had left already. Oops! I was really embarrassed about it but I knew she and I wouldn't have made it very far.

The next morning while I was at work I rang the girl up I met at the wedding and asked her out that night. She was more than happy to do meet me. The rest of the day I was just gitty like a kid wanting to get done with work which seemed to take forever for 6 pm to come around. I drove home and got ready. We were to meet at a local mall that was between us being that she lived south and I was in the north of the city. We ended up meeting next to a Starbucks that we both knew and then drove over to a restaurant called TGI Fridays. There we talked and talked and had a great time. This is also where I found out her side of the story on how we met.

She and who I thought was her mum, which was her mum, were sitting at a table with a group of old gizzers when one of them spilled her glass of wine, however not on her luckily. They had just come back from the bar when her cousin, the bride came up to the table. This gizzer told her that he had to fight the men way from her. My date said "You don't have to do that I'm looking," That is when the bride said "Oh really, I know some one else that is looking". She asked who and she said the bagpiper. She got up and said, "Well let's go and introduce me shall we."

So I was happy and that night as I kissed her and I told her that I had blind faith in this. We had a great time seeing each other one more time that week when I asked her if she was willing to go to a camping event that weekend and meet some people I know, however it had a twist, we had to dress up in costume as it was a medieval faire. She was a wee bit nervous I could see, but said why not. That weekend we both drove out to the countryside and put up a tent and changed into some medieval clothes that I had received from some friends. It was relaxing of course with tons of beer flowing around. During the day she met some interesting people. Some girls, played a joke on her during the day making her think they were lesbians and hitting on her, which seemed to put her a bit out of her element however she handle it quite well, at least I think it did. She ended up running over to me and we had a good laugh about it but wouldn't let me go to far away for a wee bit of time. I made sure she was ok and I walked over to the fake high street where the vendors where selling things. It was here that I ran into an ex girlfriend. She came up and talked to me which I really didn't care to communicate with her at all, however I'm always considerate. I was talking to her when I saw my date walk around the corner and literally push my ex out of the way and almost get into a fight. It was great to watch. Never had girls fight over me before! Well not quite that dramatic but she did nose her out of the way put her arm around me and turn me away from her leading me in another direction away from my ex.

Now I was there to provide music for the knights in battle and some entertainment during dinner. I did my job at playing during the battle which was fun to do and got dressed to go to a dinner at a friend's camp. When she and I got there the entertainment was up and going and we just joined in. I ended up playing an old Viking game called "Tublaoro", which is like chess but you use shot glasses instead and in the end everyone gets drunk, just like the Vikings. Well it took me only one game which included two beers to get me wasted so that my date ended up half carrying me to our tent. Well she pretty much had to drag me back, but we made it and before I passed out I looked at her and told her I was going to marry her. I can remember that! And then a week later I did officially ask her to be my wife and our lives have been wonderful since.

IN THE END, THERE IS ONLY ME

In doing weddings, parties or anything military whether I have played with a band or on my own the highlight and memories of my career that I have shared here are all because of my loved for playing this instrument from the day I picked it up. For some reason it takes the stress out of my life. So many events have touched my life through joy and sorrow however there have been moments in my career where nature and time just seems to stop giving me clear meaning to everything that my career has stood for.

This first event was a wedding that I did while I was up at a golf course in Seattle. It happened the day after 9/11, a fireman and his bride were getting married up at the main room of the club. When they found out that I was the bagpiper of the course they asked me to play while some pictures were getting done. As I played on the hill with the wedding couple standing at the bottom and the wind blowing around us, in that moment time had perfect meaning for me as the wind carried my music in such a perfect tribute to all. The pictures that were taken of us made a beautiful memory. Most people that were there came and talked to me after I played and told me how great it was for me to play especially on that day. Not only the couple but also the fact that I played 'Amazing Grace' for the fallen in New York City which they asked me to play after their pictures were done. Not since then, has anything so memorable been done up at that golf course according to the Seattle Times newspaper who interviewed me later.

Recently I had to play for two family funerals and though the funerals weren't fun, it reminded me that I forgot to write something at the end of my stories. Over the years when I've played and it only happens when I'm playing by myself and not with a band. But I'll be standing there playing and I'll look out the window or look across the lawn or hills of heather and see that nature has come to a stand still. Yes it's like time stops for me. Birds will hang in the air looking at me, my dog will be singing perfectly to my tunes, the squirrels will be sitting up. Even bees and bugs will not bother me and just hang loose by me. I don't know how to explain it, but it's the most beautiful and one of the biggest mysteries of things I've ever seen or heard. My wife told me once that every time you see a hummingbird that's her grandmother coming by to say hi to her. They seem to stop moving, frozen in time at moments when I'm playing. Once I had up to four sitting right in front of me for what seems like forever. Maybe something is telling me that I'm in perfect harmony with nature finely or that I'm playing for someone or something that knows I'm performing for them. It's kind of creepy really but in the end I love playing this great instrument and I plan to keep playing for years to come.

CPSIA information can be obtained at www.ICGtesting.com
Printed in the USA
BVOW071905060512

289470BV00003B/3/P